Chapters 1-16 employ fictitious characters and events to illustrate examples of stalking, harassment, and Internet trolling. Any resemblance to actual persons, living or dead, or actual events is purely coincidental.

This book is not intended to diagnose or treat any physical or mental illness or injury. The information offered is not medical or psychiatric advice, and does not replace the need for medical and/or mental health care.

ISBN-13: 979-8-9873389-1-9

Design and layout by John Combest

Printed in the United States of America

For John, Alexis and Charlotte

CONTENTS

PREFACE

I can't do this anymore.

I'm done.

I give up. He won.

"I'm gonna walk down the hall," I say quickly, over my shoulder, as I head toward the door. I try to appear confident, but my voice betrays me. I take one last look at my youngest daughter, nestled in Mommy's arms in the hospital bed, blissfully unaware of what Daddy is dealing with.

My daughter is two days old and was just subjected to her first online attack. Collateral damage of a strike aimed at me.

My kids will be okay without me, I tell myself.

I can't do this anymore.

I'm done.

He won.

I got help, that day. In that hospital.

First therapy, "Footsteps," "The Serenity Prayer." Momentary relief to get me off the ledge.

Then anguish, shame, torture, rage.

Then release, joy, acceptance, peace, love.

Today - purpose.

You're reading the book I wish I had in 2017.

◆◆◆

This book is not about ***my*** experience being stalked and harassed. It's about **yours**.

Therapists, counselors, and clergy apply the mantra, "Meet them where they are." A clinical psychologist can wax poetic about finding peace, but when a patient is in the throes of torment, aspirational lectures fall on deaf anguished ears. Useless.

This guide promises to meet you where you are. From the early shock of the attack to the lingering trauma. Because there are only three outcomes.

The first is why you bought this book. It's staying alive and becoming whole. It's the outcome you can achieve if you follow the steps laid out in the following chapters.

The second is a life of torment. Daily mental meanderings down the same monotonous and tortuous path of anxiety, fear, regret, and shame. Retraumatizing yourself. Desperately hoping and blindly groping for change that never comes. You might be on that path right now.

The third is self-deletion.

I was on the third path in 2017. I traversed the second path for years, toiling in anguish, trying to force my brain into "peace" and "acceptance" without the skills or capacity to do so. And I write this firmly ensconced on the first path.

When you bought this book, you took the first step toward

the high road. In the next chapter, we'll discuss exactly how to apply the steps to get there.

HOW TO USE (AND RE-USE) THIS GUIDE

You're at war.

That's what it feels like.

In the Preface you heard about ***a path*** to a better psychological place. And in the next chapter you'll learn about ***a ladder*** of emotions.

But right now, those pleasant analogies might seem too optimistic.

Because you're at war.

You're at war with your stalker/harasser/Internet trolls.

You're at war with your own labyrinth brain and its chambers of despair, shame, anxiety, and pain.

You may even feel like you're in a cold war with passive friends, family, classmates, or co-workers.

War is hell, but it doesn't have to be chaos.

You have a process, a battle plan.

The OODA Loop

United States Air Force Colonel John Boyd developed a decision-making process called the OODA loop.

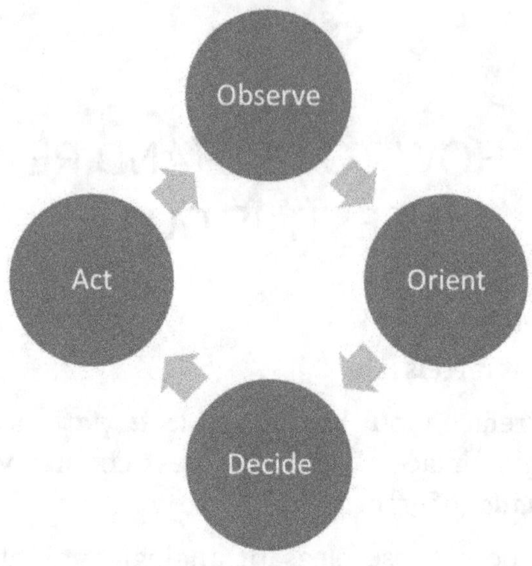

Boyd created this process for air combat, and today its influence extends far beyond the military.

When we're being attacked, our first instinct is to adopt a foxhole mentality – digging in, ducking and covering, literally shrinking to avoid the next onslaught. This ground-warfare viewpoint can be overcome by an air-strike mentality.

As such, this book is organized in OODA loop fashion.

Observe

In the first six chapters, you'll observe six people dealing with stalkers, harassers, and Internet trolls.

You'll watch as each person reacts to the attacks upon them, and you'll learn to identify the range of emotions most of us experience when we're under siege.

Depending upon the type of harassment you're dealing with, you might relate to some or all the fictional situations in the first six chapters. As such, you'll find yourself evaluating how each of the protagonists reacts to their individual situation, and you'll have the opportunity to capture those observations at the end of each chapter.

Orient

In Chapters 7 and 8, you'll orient yourself and your current mindset.

In Chapter 7, we'll go head-to-head with the exact, verbatim attacks against you to discover why they're causing you emotional pain. We'll identify self-harming core beliefs and explore how our stalkers, harassers and Internet trolls exploit those beliefs to inflict emotional pain.

In Chapter 8, we'll continue to directly address the attacks against us – this time, through the lens of our core human wants. You'll learn how our universal desires for control, security and approval are at the root of our anxieties about being attacked, and you'll learn how to identify and begin freeing yourself from each core want.

Decide

With the knowledge gained from observing others (Chapters 1-6) and orienting your own belief system (Chapters 7-8), it's decision time.

Do you want to let go of the painful past? Or do you wish to stay hunkered in your foxhole?

The decision is not as clear-cut as it may seem. In Chapter 9 you'll learn why you're tempted to stay where you are, physically and mentally, in the mistaken belief that you're protecting yourself. You'll face up to any underlying desires to be a "permavictim" and conquer those weaknesses before moving forward.

Act

Having made a conscious commitment to improve your situation and regain control of your mind, it's time to act.

We'll give a name to our collective stalkers/harassers/ Internet trolls based on their five key characteristics/traits. We'll discuss each of those traits, and the psychological traps that can ensnare us.

For each poisonous characteristic, we'll name the antidote – and give specific steps to overcome the pain inflicted by our stalkers and even by ourselves.

Format and Style

This guide was written in a style that enables you to read it – and put it into use – as quickly as possible.

As a result, big ideas and key themes from seminal books – including Hale Dwoskin's The Sedona Method, JF Benoist's Addicted to the Monkey Mind: Change the Programming that Sabotages Your Life and Joe Dispenza's Breaking the Habit of Being Yourself are summarized succinctly, with additional context and links provided in footnotes.

We'll use proper nouns for the levels of emotions, and acronyms for our collective stalkers.

Journaling

Capturing your thoughts in real time is a critical part of recovering and rebuilding from online attacks. Your brain is building new neural pathways as your read and reflect on the skills presented in this book. **You cannot rely on memory alone.** Use a traditional notebook or, in a pinch, a digital note-taking tool for the exercises marked "Journal" at the end of each chapter.

Disclaimer

Chapters 1-16 employ fictitious characters and events to illustrate examples of stalking, harassment, and Internet trolling. Any resemblance to actual persons, living or dead, or actual events is purely coincidental.

This book is not intended to diagnose or treat any physical or mental illness or injury. The information offered is not medical or psychiatric advice, and does not replace the need for medical and/or mental health care.

Trademarks

Facebook and Instagram are trademarks of Meta.

Twitter and "tweet" are trademarks of Twitter.

Google, "googles" and YouTube are trademarks of Google LLC.

Tinder is the exclusive registered trademark of Match Group, LLC.

The Sedona Method ® is a trademarked process.

Safety

If you believe you are being stalked, and/or you or someone close to you is being threatened, contact law enforcement authorities in your jurisdiction.

In the United States, the National Domestic Violence Hotline phone number is 1-800-799-7233 (SAFE). The group also provides a Stalking Safety Planning guide at www.thehotline.org.

The Stalking Prevention, Awareness, & Resource Center (SPARC) provides education and resources about the crime of stalking. Visit www.stalkingawareness.org.

CHAPTER 1: OBSERVE: KAREN'S APATHY

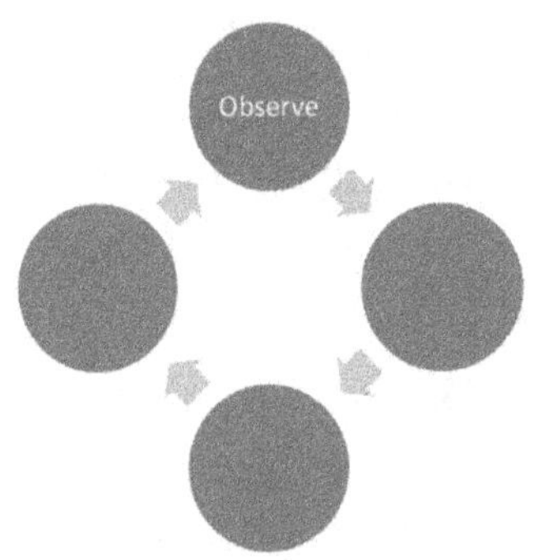

> Inherent in all of us are nine emotional states: apathy, grief, fear, lust, anger, pride, courageousness, acceptance, and peace ... These fall along a gradient scale of energy and action. In apathy, we have almost no energy available to us and take little or no external action. We have more energy and take more action when we move up to grief. Each successive emotion in this scale, all the way up to peace, has more energy and affords us a greater capability for outward action.[1]

Meet Karen. She is a wife, and a mother, and was until recently a supervisor at a retail supercenter. During the COVID-19 pandemic, she was on the front lines of enforcing her store's mask rules. The worst part of her job, she felt, was mediating the occasional arguments between shoppers over the store's mask requirement.

One morning when attempting to resolve a dispute between two shoppers over proper mask placement, Karen snapped. She told one of the shoppers to "suck it up" and "pull it (the mask) up." She even let out a guttural yell/moan in frustration before the shoppers went their separate ways. As Karen stormed off to the break room to cool down, she was already filling out the company's standard "Incident Report" in her mind and putting her best spin on her loss of control.

What Karen didn't know was that one of the shopper's friends recorded the incident on their phone, and within hours had posted an edited version of the video to Facebook, Twitter and Instagram.

Before Karen had even completed the company's incident form that afternoon, she received an email from her manager. The company's social media team had flagged the posts, activating the "crisis management team" from corporate headquarters.

Karen pled her case to the Human Resources group supervisor the next day, but to no avail. Karen was terminated.

The attacks

Two weeks after she was dismissed, Karen is still stuck. Her husband and her kids see her performing her usual tasks around the house, but she's not the same wife and mother she was before her viral "Karen moment." Her husband encourages her to talk about her feelings, but Karen shuts down the conversation each time. Her kids fear that any mention of the video and ensuing fallout will set her off.

During the COVID pandemic, Karen's primary method of keeping in touch with friends and family was through Facebook. In fact, she preferred the ease of posting, replying, and messaging to the logistics and effort involved in in-person conversations or talking on the phone. But the incident at work changed Karen's relationship with social media. Her accounts get tagged every time someone posts a "Karen Meltdown Remix" or a similar mockery, and someone even posted a photo of Karen's home from a real estate database website. (Karen flagged that post for harassment, and it was taken down.)

And that's not Karen's only newfound hangup with social media. The last time she logged in, she headed straight to her direct messages to glean a few supporting messages from friends.

"Hang in there, girl," Karen expected to see.

"Don't let this craziness get you down!" she thought she'd receive in the inbox.

But there were no such pick-me-ups awaiting her. None.

Karen tells her family that her top priority is finding a new job. But when her husband leaves the house for work and the kids are at school, Karen can't seem to get herself off the couch. The heaviness of her sudden unemployment, and her new status as an online punchline, feel like a lead blanket pinning her to the sofa cushions.

Today

Most days, Karen does in fact manage to get off the couch, open her laptop, and go through the motions of job hunting. But as she scrolls the available opportunities, her mind fast-forwards to a hypothetical job interview.

"Why did you leave your last job?" the fictional hiring manager asks in Karen's mind, and Karen is paralyzed. Did the hiring manager Google her name? Was he one of the thousands of people who retweeted the video of her tirade? Is he just messing with her, and wants to see how she'll respond?

While Karen's conscious mind knows she's at home sitting at her computer, her unconscious mind and sympathetic nervous system are sitting in the make-believe job interview. Karen feels her heart race and a lump grow in her throat.[2]

The fight-or-flight instinct has kicked in, and Karen feels like she has no more fight left in her. She closes the laptop, gets up from her chair, and heads to the kitchen for a drink.

Listen to yourself

If our emotional states were a ladder, apathy would be the bottom rung. When we're in this state, we feel powerless to change our situation. We feel like expending any effort is a waste of time.

When we're stuck in apathy, our self-talk sounds like this:

"It's no use."

"It doesn't even matter."

"There's no point in even trying."

When others reach out to help, offering encouragement and hope, we attempt to dissuade them. We want them, too, to believe our situation is hopeless.

Journal

For many of us, our initial reaction to being stalked,

harassed, or trolled is Anger. When we realize that the consequences of the harassment may involve losing our jobs, family or friends, our minds quickly slip down the ladder of emotions and bottom out in Apathy.

Was there a point in which you felt Apathy's hopelessness and futility? When did you first notice it?

Write it down in your Journal. We'll dive deeper into those feelings, and their underlying assumptions and expectations, in Chapters 7-8.

CHAPTER 2: OBSERVE: LISA'S GRIEF

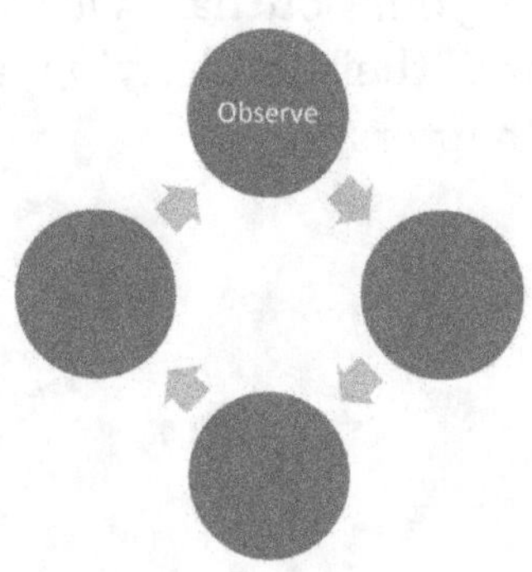

Lisa, 42, lost her husband Scott to COVID-related illness nine months ago. Scott had survived serious health challenges over the previous decade – he was more than 20 years older than Lisa – and each medical procedure took an incremental toll on his body. Despite this – or perhaps because of it – Scott's optimism shone even brighter. Lisa saw him as her inspiration to look on the bright side during the darkest of times.

The profound loss of her husband would have remained a private matter among Lisa's family and friends, but there were two catches – Lisa was a city councilwoman, and Scott worked in a separate local government department. When asked by local media whether she had been vaccinated against COVID, Lisa answered truthfully. She said that both she and Scott had concerns about what they considered the experimental nature of the COVID vaccines, and after talking with their family physician, they both chose to decline the inoculation.

When Scott was first admitted to the hospital with COVID, Lisa's local political detractors gleefully amplified news reports of the hospitalization. Social media messages echoed a similar theme: "He's getting what he deserves," the kneejerk critics tweeted and posted. Lisa couldn't help but see these angry missives – the trolls had tagged her in most of the posts – but with Scott bedridden on a ventilator, she had the center of her figurative universe to literally lean upon.

Eventually, Scott succumbed to the illness. Lisa posted an old picture of her and Scott, along with a brief message, on her social media accounts to let family and friends know that Scott had passed. Lisa's phone notifications began popping up immediately with texts, Twitter direct messages and private Facebook messages from friends and acquaintances offering their condolences.

Then the trolls arrived.

The attacks

Most trolls hid behind anonymous accounts with no names attached. They mocked Scott's weight, his age, his religion, even his well-regarded sense of humor – nothing seemed to be off limits. Some who identified as agnostic or atheist in their Twitter profiles said that Scott was rotting in hell. That dichotomy was an irony in which Scott would have found humor, but in the moment, it was no laughing matter for Lisa.

Some trolls went so far as to theorize that Lisa pressured Scott into declining the COVID vaccine to further her political credentials if she ran for higher office. It was a ridiculous assertion, but especially hurtful because the intent was seemingly to blame Lisa for Scott's death.

Lisa didn't mind being criticized for her political views. Prior to her election, she spent years volunteering for candidates and causes and knew that politics was a rough-and-tumble business. But these attacks were more about personality than policy.

Today

Lisa was overwhelmed by the turnout at Scott's memorial service. Hundreds of friends traveled from across the country to pay their respects to Scott and to comfort Lisa. But in the nine months that have passed, the supportive texts and calls have grown fewer and far between. Meanwhile, the online ridicule has only partially subsided. Each time news outlets report a high-profile COVID casualty of an unvaccinated person, a fresh wave of Facebook posts link to online news reports of Scott's death.

It's easy for most of us reading about Lisa's loss to identify – or at least anticipate – that she was experiencing grief. But Lisa's social media trolls are throwing what seem to be permanent monkey wrenches in the typical grieving pathway from early disbelief and shock to eventual peace.

Burying herself into her work as a public servant offers no respite for Lisa. Both her official government e-mail account, as well as her political campaign account, receive a slow but steady stream of hateful messages. In the first week after Scott's death, the messages were nearly 50-50 belittling vs. supportive; today, that ratio is roughly 95-5 in favor of the trolls.

Like Karen in Chapter 1, Lisa is choosing to drastically minimize her use of social media. This decision shields her from the barrage of hateful memes but it also cuts off some points of contact with an extensive support network. Even before running for elective office, Lisa was a virtual one-woman information hub for countless friends. She communicated with many of them through Twitter direct messages and Facebook Messenger. She uses those tools far less frequently today.

Moreover, Lisa has begun to wonder why so few of her political friends and acquaintances have fought back in her defense against the trolls. Surely, they see the tweets and posts too. Lisa reasons that she could track down the identity of several of the meme-makers. In fact, some nights she has stayed up late to do just that.

"Where are my friends to take up this battle with me?" she asks herself each day. She sees her political allies and fellow elected officials going about their usual business, writing and publishing fluffy op-eds and "constituent reports" as if the world isn't off its axis. Don't they see she's in pain?

Listen to yourself

When we're stuck in grief, our self-talk sounds like this:

"They forgot about me."

"Can't they see how much I'm hurting?"

"Nobody cares."

Journal

At some point in being stalked, harassed or trolled, have you felt like your friends and family abandoned you? Do you feel as if no one realizes or acknowledges the pain and suffering you've endured?

Capture those uncensored feelings in your journal. We'll identify their source in Chapters 7-8, and how to address absentee "friends" in Chapter 15.

CHAPTER 3: OBSERVE: ALYSSA'S FEAR

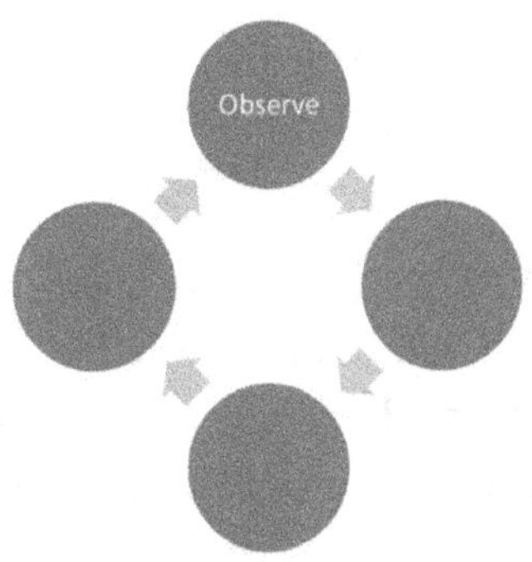

Alyssa H., 24, is an accounts supervisor at a global public relations firm. She's single, having recently broken up with James, her on-again-off-again boyfriend. He stayed behind in their mid-size college town when Alyssa moved to the big city, and James grew increasingly insecure about her new life and the men she was meeting through work and social activities. His weak, insolent disposition was a far cry from the secure confidence he demonstrated before she moved, and Alyssa felt herself outgrowing James.

Alyssa was proud of how she conducted herself the day of their breakup – implementing advice from her therapist, she had a direct, compassionate, and non-dramatic conversation with James. She even held out hope that despite his initial tears and pleading, she and James could be long-distance friends one day.

Two months after the breakup, Alyssa spent a Friday evening at home sipping a glass of wine and vanity-searching her name on Google. As she hoped, the first page of results included her PR firm's projects and highlighted her contributions. A rosé-fueled warmth filled her cheeks. But when she got to the bottom of the first page of search results, her heart jumped into her throat.

The attack

"ALYSSA H____ EXPOSED" the search result screamed. She clicked on the link and was taken to a site where users post explicit photos and videos. Someone posted dozens of pictures of Alyssa with suggestive captions. She recognized the pictures immediately as ones she had texted to James when they were dating. The anonymous user added the name of her employer, and even her work e-mail address.

Alyssa burst into tears – and as she threw her body down onto the sofa, her mind began careening down rungs of the emotional ladder from the Courage and Acceptance she felt just moments ago, lower and lower into Anger and Fear.

While Karen (Chapter 1) and Lisa (Chapter 2) were mired in Apathy and Grief, respectively, Alyssa was feeling Fear. Fear provides more energy than the two lower-frequency emotions.

That sense of Fear powered Alyssa through the first sleepless evening to write a "rapid response plan", much like her company did for corporate clients. Though her mind and body were being flooded with endorphins, her crisis plan was clinical and tactical, focused on reputation management and legal options.

Alyssa texted James in the morning. Predictably, he denied posting the photos. He even claimed he had taken his phone to a shopping mall kiosk to fix a cracked screen and speculated someone at the repair store must have downloaded the photos. Plausible deniability. But James couldn't give Alyssa the name of the supposed phone-repair kiosk, and Alyssa cut the conversation short.

Burying her emotions that morning, Alyssa prioritized "reputation management." Through her college and professional training, she was well-versed on search-engine optimization principles, and knew that some companies could clean up search engine results for a fee. But those services were expensive, and none were foolproof.

Exploring legal options was her second priority. On this topic, Alyssa was much less knowledgeable. She remembered skimming online magazine articles about young women dealing with so-called "revenge porn," and how some victims had tried to sue their exes or have the photo and video files removed from websites. Alyssa also knew that image-hosting websites often had so-called mirror sites to replicate files across the world, virtually ensuring a photo or video never truly went away.

She did not remember how those stories ended – although she did remember thinking those women were foolish for sharing intimate photos with their partners in the first place and pitied their poor judgement.

Today

Alyssa is three months removed from her discovery of the image-hosting site, and she has made modest progress on her initial rapid-response plan. She reached out to three reputation-management firms and found their quoted fees to be far out of her budget. Alyssa attempted a do-it-yourself approach, implementing tips she gleaned from online sources and her own company's internal training guides for SEO specialists. After adding some plain-Jane profiles to highly trafficked websites, Alyssa saw the "ALYSSA H___ EXPOSED" search result drop down to the second page of Google results for her first and last name.[3]

Alyssa checks the search-engine results with multiple keyword combinations each day. The ritualistic behavior makes her feel like she is in control and helps bury her emotions about James and his anonymous revenge posting site. But underneath her self-soothing compulsive behavior is a sensitive layer of fear.

Alyssa wonders: What if a curious co-worker or client googles her and makes it to the second page of Google results? There's no denying her face in some of the photos. All it would take is one e-mail from a stranger – or James himself – to her company, linking to the image site, and her professional world would come crashing down around her.

Listen to yourself

When we're trapped in fear, our self-talk sounds like:

"They're going to find out – what will I say when they mention it?"

"They're looking at me funny. I bet they already know."

"I've got to lay low until I get this all figured out."

Journal

While being stalked and/or harassed, when did you first notice yourself feeling fearful of consequences out of your control? Are those feelings recurring to this day?

Do you worry about being "found out" or "exposed" due to the actions of a malevolent actor like James? Do you feel like you will somehow be punished for your stalker/harasser/Internet troll's behavior?

Make note of those thoughts in your journal, and we'll explore them further in Chapters 7-8.

CHAPTER 4: OBSERVE: TYLER'S LUST

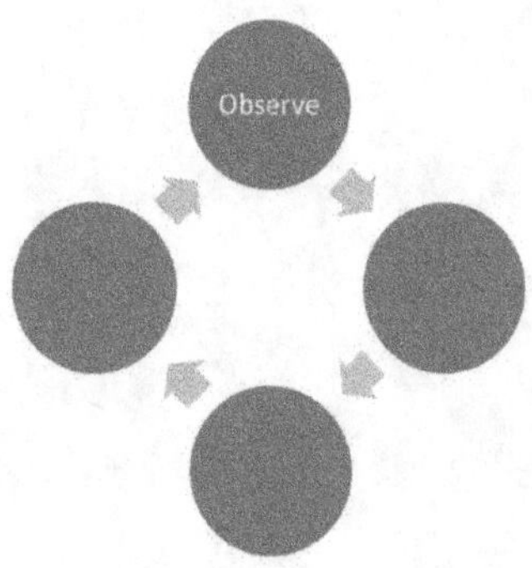

Tyler, 27, is single and works as a business reporter for the daily newspaper in a mid-sized U.S. city. His path to the current gig followed the time-honored journalism duo of dogged determination and lucky breaks.

Tyler started as a stringer in his college days, which helped him nab a job as a general assignment reporter after he graduated from journalism school. When the reporter covering local government retired, Tyler was promoted to the politics beat. Two years later, a newspaper in the same corporate conglomerate had an opening for a business reporter, and Tyler was recruited for the position. The job interview was a mere formality, but Tyler prepared diligently and was elated to begin his work.

The first attack

No sooner had Tyler published his debut business-beat piece – a seemingly innocuous story about redevelopment of downtown warehouses – did the city's nabob of negativity appear on the scene. In a bygone era, Dan Andrews would have been called a gadfly or simply a pest, but in the modern world he was considered a Twitter troll. Labeling the paper's new hire "Tyler the Toady," Dan tweeted that Tyler was already being manipulated by one of the city's top political and media consultants.

That allegation was preposterous to Tyler, who had never met, spoken with, or even exchanged emails with the consultant. From what Tyler gathered by scrolling through Dan's Twitter feed, Dan possessed both encyclopedic knowledge of the city's leadership figures *and* grudges against many of those leaders. Tyler did not reply to the initial tweet; in fact, no one replied to it or favorited it. That was common – though hundreds in the city's business and political circles read Dan's tweets, few chose to directly engage with him.

Deep down, being added to Dan's extensive enemies list made Tyler feel significant. Even if the "in-group" was primarily virtual, at least it was a welcoming tribe in an unfamiliar city. Other people who had been targeted by Dan's tweets sent Tyler direct messages welcoming him to the informal club and telling him not to worry about Dan.

Tyler felt like he was the protagonist in a teen coming-of-age movie – walking into a crowded lunchroom with no place to sit, getting rudely pushed by the school's bully, then having the popular crowd – jocks (politicians), high achievers (entrepreneurs) and cheerleaders (reporters) – immediately ask him to sit with them at their lunch table.

Tyler had found his virtual spot.

The counter-attacks

One month into the new gig, Tyler attended the soft launch of a startup brewery in one of the refurbished downtown warehouses. The happy hour drew the city's top civic leaders and entrepreneur types, and it was the first opportunity Tyler had to meet many of those personalities in person.

When Tyler returned home that evening, he opened his phone's Twitter app to find more than a dozen notifications that he had been tagged in photos. Dan Andrews was on a tweetstorm about the event, having watched the brewery's Instagram Live video of the founder's welcome speech. Dan was posting screenshots, with creative text captions imagining what "Tyler the Toady" and other attendees had been saying to each other.

Tyler had had enough. Maybe it was ego, maybe it was a desire to strike a blow on behalf of the cool crowd, maybe it was the free IPAs he threw back at the brewery – whatever it was, a switch flipped in Tyler's mind that convinced him to strike back. Tyler booted up his personal laptop and within a few minutes had created his own "sock puppet" account to troll Dan, at "@DanAndys."

Over the next several weeks, Tyler used the DanAndys account to take daily pokes at Dan. DanAndys started with feigned praise for Dan's conspiracy theories and sprinkled in some red herrings designed to waste Dan's time. The real Dan eventually blocked the DanAndys account from viewing updates, but Tyler (through his legit public account) could still view the real Dan's Twitter posts and capture screenshots of tweets and replies.

Whereas Dan's tweets received little engagement, DanAndys' follower count grew steadily each week. And when Tyler's alt account started posting photos of Dan gleaned from Facebook, putting Dan's image into his own clever memes, they got double-digit retweets and likes.

Tyler felt himself falling deeper in love with his Twitter alter ego each day. The business beat had reignited his fiery passion for journalism, and this kabuki-like battle with Dan threw fresh fuel on the flames. After two months on the job, Tyler was still outperforming at work by every metric that mattered, and his editor was pleased. But Tyler spent nearly as much time thinking about his DanAndys account as he spent working on news stories. He had even created a second sock-puppet account to heckle Dan in a different voice and tone.

Today

As Tyler's anti-Dan memes and tweets grow more caustic and biting, Dan's reactive posts become more serious and intense. As such, Tyler is necessarily investing more deeply in his rationalizations for trolling.

Dan is a nuisance to good people, Tyler tells himself, and by wasting Dan's time the DanAndys account is serving the greater good. Besides, it's about time somebody struck back against media critics. For too long, local journalists have been painted with a broad brush by critics of "the media" and it's time somebody stood up for the profession.

Trolling the troll makes Tyler feel more alive than ever, but there are opportunity costs. For starters, Tyler has abandoned his plans to join a gym in his new city. He had envisioned prioritizing his health, as many of his workaholic journalism colleagues neglect to do, and now he had fallen into the same trap as the others.

Tyler compartmentalizes his trolling time by working diligently on his real work throughout the day and only logging into his DanAndys account before work, at lunchtime and after work. But this means that he passes up healthy socializing with co-workers after office hours, preferring instead to settle in at home with fast food or takeout and his laptop to keep the DanAndys momentum moving.

Tyler's most disturbing realization is that he is starting to see the world through Dan's eyes. From his colleagues' self-congratulatory messages and vanity tweets to the banal gibber of local business leaders, Tyler is starting to mentally reframe local happenings as Dan might see them.

"He can't be right about all that stuff – can he?" Tyler wonders.

Tyler never identified as obsessive-compulsive, but he recognizes that he is obsessed with Dan - and that his DanAndys scheming is compulsive behavior. I'll quit, he tells himself, when Dan Andrews finally learns his lesson.

Listen to yourself

When we are stuck in lust, our self-talk sounds like this:

"I've got to have it."

"More, more, more!"

"I'm not obsessed, I'm just driven."

Journal

Have you ever plotted revenge against your stalker, harasser or Internet troll?

Have you taken steps to enact revenge – fake social

media accounts, "sock puppet" profiles, anonymous e-mail accounts?

How did it feel when you were taking these actions? Did you feel like you were striking a blow for righteousness? What other rationalizations did you make to explain away your deceptive/deceitful behavior?

Did you ever feel as though your quest for more – more revenge, more retribution – was ever fully satiated?

CHAPTER 5: OBSERVE: KEITH'S ANGER

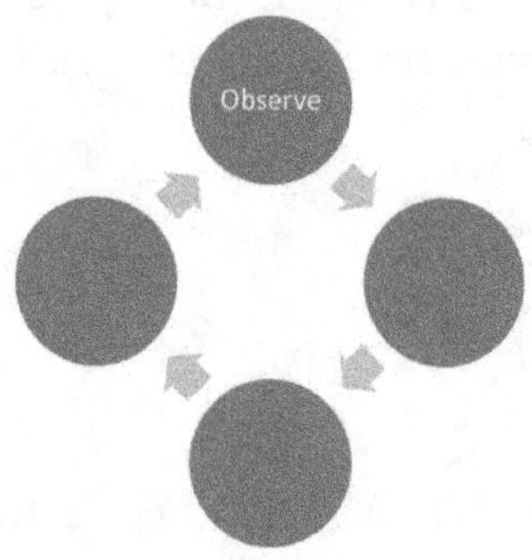

Keith, 52, is married and has two teenage children at home. He leads a software engineering team at a global financial services company based in New York City.

When he was in his early 30s, Keith created a hobby blog focused on the booming online payments industry. Writing the blog brought Keith great joy, and its success opened doors to relationships in the industry – ultimately leading to his current finance gig.

A few months after Keith started his website, an acquaintance named Chris started a blog of his own. Chris used his blog to promote conspiracy theories involving the global monetary system. Keith gave Chris blogging advice when asked, even though one-world conspiracy rantings were a bit out of Keith's wheelhouse.

Keith's blog quickly became a must-visit site for a niche group of finance professionals, and Chris grew increasingly resentful of Keith's success. Chris felt that Keith wasn't doing nearly enough to promote Chris' conspiracy-theory blog.

The first round of attacks

One day, Chris went ballistic – he sent Keith a profanity-laced e-mail from an anonymous account, but the message revealed his IP address and Chris confessed to writing the hateful screed. Months later, Chris created an anonymous "Mobile Payment News Service" website dedicated to harassing Keith.

Keith did his best to avoid instigating Chris, but ignoring the online harassment was hard. When Keith's mother died, Chris posted a sarcastic "condolence" message to the anti-Keith hate blog. When Keith's father died two years later, Chris seemed to once again revel in Keith's pain and posted a similar missive.

Keith knew his former acquaintance was hurting. For starters, Chris had quit his full-time job to spite his ex-wife and child, who relied on Chris' child support payments to make ends meet. After Chris started an off-the-books hustle peddling grey-market "investments," the state's securities division won a court judgment for tens of thousands of dollars. Eventually, Chris stole thousands of dollars from his own mother, who filed a lawsuit against Chris to recoup some of the stolen funds. Retired and living on a small pension, Chris' mother was heartbroken to find out the money Chris had stolen was long gone, and she mercifully dropped the case against him.

While Keith knew Chris was in pain, he recoiled at the thought of reaching out to his former acquaintance. Besides, Keith had more pressing issues to attend to – he got arrested for driving while intoxicated.

Keith had been working in his backyard garden one Sunday afternoon when he realized the beer he was sipping – his third that session – was his last. He jumped in his truck and drove to the massive superstore a few miles down the road.

Keith rolled through a stop sign pulling into the store parking lot, and his heart jumped into his throat when he saw a police cruiser flash its lights and pull in behind his truck. Keith was arrested for drinking and driving.

Within hours, the case appeared on the state's court database website. Chris signed up for database email alerts years prior, which would be triggered if Keith's name ever appeared in the database. After years of digging around in the mud, Chris had finally struck paydirt with something of substance to post on his hate blog.

The second round of attacks

"DRUNK DRIVER ARRESTED AFTER DAYTIME BENDER" the headline on the hate blog blared. Chris had waited to post the news until Keith's first appearance in court. Chris wanted to inflict the maximum amount of emotional pain possible upon Keith, and the morning of the court date was the opportune time.

Chris used his anonymous "Mobile Payment News Service" Twitter account to tweet out the DWI story. To ramp up the sense of alarm, Chris tagged Keith's friends, employer, and even local journalists in a series of tweets that morning.

While Keith's friends were aware of his stalker, the executives of his company were not. He told the company's

HR department about the DWI arrest the day after it happened – but how was he supposed to explain Chris' hate blog? What if someone thought Chris' "Mobile Payment News Service" was an actual media site with credibility?

Today

"Why are my friends taking this so lightly?" Keith asks himself. His friends see the hate-blog post as simply another iteration of Chris' creepy obsession. But to Keith, it was much bigger than the previous gloating posts about his parents' deaths. By tagging Keith's company and co-workers in social media posts, Chris was attacking Keith's livelihood.

Fuming, Keith has composed a few blog post titles of his own in his head. "Cowardly Deadbeat Attacks Family Breadwinner." "Child-Abandoning Grifter Hits Gossip Jackpot." Like Tyler (Chapter 4), Keith imagines creating his own anonymous Twitter accounts to attack Chris.

While the legal issues involving the DWI are clear-cut and linear, Keith's retaliatory rage against Chris is not. It seems he can feel his blood boiling just under the surface of his skin, and he wonders if his heart rate will ever return to normal.

Listen to yourself

When we are mired in anger, our self-talk sounds like:

"I'm going to make him pay."

"They're going to regret what they've done to me."

"I'll get my revenge and destroy everything important to her."

Journal

From the moment you were first attacked until today, what are some of the destructive thoughts Anger has brought to your consciousness?

Have you thought about taking revenge on your stalker?

Have you thought about taking drastic actions – including bodily harm – to put an end to your stalker's behavior?

Have you taken any steps to put those revenge plans into action?

CHAPTER 6: OBSERVE: GABBY'S PRIDE

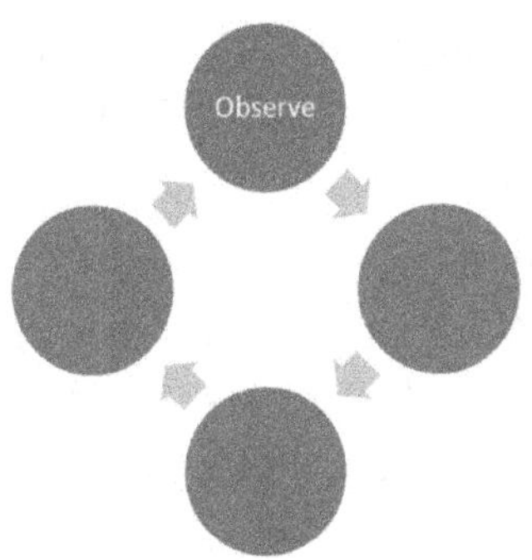

Gabby, 38, is the president of the transit authority of a fast-growing metropolitan U.S. region. Gabby studied civil engineering in college, then was admitted straight from undergrad into a Doctor of Philosophy in Civil and Environmental Engineering (Ph.D.) program.

Gabby was the first in her family to graduate from college, and she was the only African-American female in her undergrad civil engineering and Ph.D. graduating classes. She was embarrassingly self-conscious about looking different from her classmates in the earliest days of her undergraduate experience. But it didn't take long until she "flipped the script," as she liked to say, and began embracing how distinctly she stood out from the typical male 'engi-nerd' crowd.

After earning her Ph.D., Gabby joined a Fortune 500 civil engineering firm. She was promoted multiple times before being recruited by the transit authority board. Taking the new job meant a pay cut from her hefty private-sector salary, but the role would give Gabby a voice in how federal infrastructure funds would be spent in the region. This was bigger than just designing and funding roads – for Gabby, it could mean building a more equitable transportation system for her community.

In much the same way as Tyler's new gig earned him the scorn of a gadfly, Gabby's position put her in the crosshairs of the mayor's political enemies. Kelley Lynn called herself a "legal eagle" on Twitter, but she behaved more like a cackling vulture.

Kelley had been a top campaign consultant to the previous mayor, who went to jail for accepting bribes in exchange for city contracts. Gabby's now-boss won a special election to replace the corrupt mayor.

In dramatic fashion, Kelley Lynn abruptly distanced herself from the previous mayor and became her region's self-appointed Twitter lawyer for ethical topics.[4]

Meanwhile, civic leaders saw the influx of federal infrastructure money as an opportunity to improve the region's transit system and boost the local economy. Kelley Lynn viewed the cash infusion opportunistically as well. She planned to use her sizable Twitter following to advance the false rumor that the current administration, including Gabby, was handing out big-money contracts to political cronies instead of the most qualified bidders.

To Gabby, a political neophyte, that notion was ridiculous.

Throughout her private-sector career, she had spent thousands of hours poring over government agencies' requests for proposals (RFPs) and preparing her firm's submissions. Sure, there were always rumors that certain RFPs were "wired" or slanted to favor one bidder or another. But every engineering firm knew that even the appearance of wasteful spending, fraud or grift could do irreparable damage to the company's reputation and endanger future bids.

In much the same way that Dan Andrews sought to instigate Tyler (Chapter 4), Kelley Lynn took aim at Gabby. While Dan's attacks on Tyler were executed in a chaotic and shotgun-like manner, Kelley's approach was more methodical and thematic. Like a musical composer, Kelley orchestrated a plan to layer one melody on top of another, each addition harmonizing with the ones laid prior.

The first line of attack would undermine Gabby's qualifications. Kelley planned to retweet every local news article about the massive amounts of money headed to the region, then ask rhetorically if taxpayers deserved better leadership than someone getting "on the job training" like Gabby.

The attacks

Gabby was dialed into a conference call when her #BossBabe text thread – the informal group of female leaders in the administration – lit up her phone. Gabby clicked on the text link and read Kelley Lynn's first "on the job training" tweet. Gabby reflexively covered her mouth as she whispered, "Oh my God." She felt her heart jump into her throat and her eyes well up.

Gabby was incensed not only by what Kelley said in the tweet, by also by what Gabby ***thought*** Kelley was ***really*** saying.

Ever since Gabby was hired at her previous job, she had steeled herself against the argument that she was a "diversity hire." She had African-American friends in other industries who were aggressively recruited by companies looking to diversify their workforces. Those friends privately joked with Gabby that they were all benefitting from affirmative action. Gabby feigned laughter at the remarks but was privately offended. Her civil engineering classes were not cakewalks like social sciences classes, she told herself.

"I earned my degree and I earned this job," she repeated to herself for years. Kelley's tweet didn't mention race, but it didn't matter. Deep down, Gabby felt she knew what Kelley ***really*** meant by "qualifications."

The rest of the afternoon, Gabby was tethered to her phone even more tightly than usual. She enjoyed the positive affirmations from her #BossBabe text thread. On the flip side, she obsessively reloaded Kelley's tweet, watching the number of retweets, likes and replies grow. Before leaving the office for the day, Gabby took a screenshot of the "likes" and saved it to her photo gallery. She'd remember how these people piled on, she told herself, and would throw it right back in their faces one day.

When Gabby got home from work, she recounted the day's Twitter travails to her husband Tom. As usual, Tom was disappointingly rational about Kelley Lynn.

"Who cares what that old wine hag thinks?" he asked

Gabby rhetorically. "You can't control her, and no tweets, twits or twats actually affect the work you produce every day."

"You're right, you're right," Gabby replied mechanically. "Thank you for reminding me."

Gabby changed the subject, but her mind was still anchored upon Kelley and the "qualifications" jab. Gabby obsessed over the tweet during dinner, then had an idea.

The next day, Gabby carried her framed diplomas into work and hung them on her office wall. Her office had a captivating view of the metro park, which served as a scenic backdrop when Gabby was on camera for virtual calls. But now, inspired to refute Kelley's "qualifications" tweet, Gabby had turned her desk 90 degrees to allow everyone to see her dual diplomas on the wall behind her. She even added "Ph.D." after her name in her Twitter bio.

The attacks, continued

The ostentatious display of academic credentials did not stop Kelley from banging on about Gabby's lack of qualifications. Kelley began layering on the second round of Twitter criticism, chirping that Gabby was spending quite a bit of time at civic events and not much time working on the infrastructure spending rollout.

Gabby had legitimate business reasons for attending municipal events around the region – hearing from elected officials and business owners was a key part of her job. Regardless, Kelley sought out photos from chamber of commerce luncheons, cropped the ones that included Gabby, and tweeted them with hashtags like "#Gabfest" and "#GabbyOnTheClock."

Once again, Gabby couldn't resist responding in an over-the-top manner to goad her nemesis. Gabby started attending even more chamber breakfasts and luncheons, then used her own Twitter account to tweet photos of herself socializing. Gabby relished seeing Kelley quote-tweet these posts and would send the screenshots immediately to her #BossBabe text thread. Gabby lapped up the instant validation from her friends.

The third layer of Kelley Lynn's orchestral attack sought to make Gabby hyper-aware of her own appearance. At an evening gala, Gabby wore a striking shade of red lipstick. Kelley used a tightly cropped picture with a harsh filter to create a new "#GabbyInTheRed" meme. It was a linguistic stretch, even for Kelley, but she managed to tie "in the red" to Gabby's alleged overspending. The more Kelley seemed to gaslight Gabby, the more indignant Gabby became.

Today

Gabby fashions herself an amateur psychologist and tells her #BossBabe friends that Kelley Lynn is projecting her own guilt about the previous mayor's corruption onto the current mayor's staff.

"Doesn't everybody else see that too?" Gabby asks herself.

At this moment, Kelley Lynn is actively recruiting a candidate to run against Gabby's boss in the next election. Gabby knows Kelley will turn up the frequency and intensity of trolling, hoping to press Gabby into making an unforced error.

But Gabby won't allow herself to dial down the ostentatious attitude. Doing so would appear to give Kelley Lynn a victory. Just one more coat of bright lipstick, one more hair flip for the camera, Gabby tells herself, with a sly smile for her friends cheering her on.

Listen to yourself

When we're feeling Pride, our self-talk sounds like:

"They're just jealous."

"She wishes she could be me."

"I'll be a little bit extra, just to show them who's in charge."

Journal

Do you go out of your way to spite your stalker, harasser or Internet trolls?

Do you allow the idea of taunting your Internet trolls to dominate your thoughts and actions?

If you've taken actions to appear more boastful or self-satisfied on social media, how did those actions make you feel? Were the effects on your mind short-term, long-term, both or neither?

CHAPTER 7: ORIENT: ATTACKS AND YOUR CORE BELIEFS

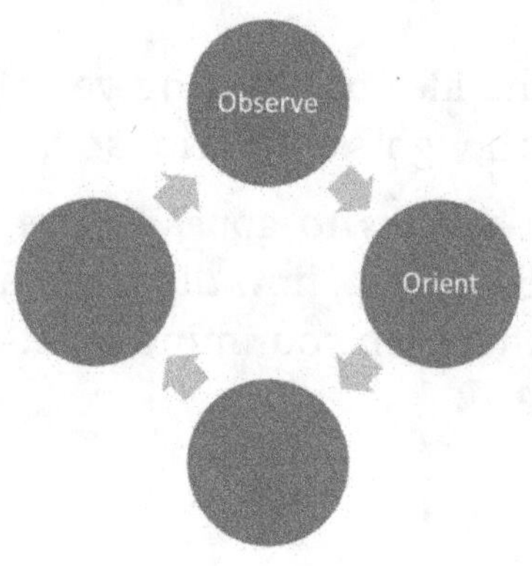

> "30. TAKING THINGS TO THEIR ILLOGICAL CONCLUSION
>
> Example: If you let your barber cut your hair, the next thing you know he'll be lopping off your limbs!" – Scott Adams[5]

It's easy to laugh at other peoples' irrational thought processes, like this example provided by Dilbert creator Scott Adams. But it's harder for us to identify our own illogical leaps, particularly when they're part of the mental pathways our brains have mapped and traveled for decades.

In the first six chapters, we **Observed** six emotional levels of reactions to stalkers, harassers and Internet trolls.

In this chapter, you'll learn how to **Orient** your current belief system in relation to attacks from your stalkers, harassers and Internet trolls, as well as your own illogical conclusions.

Together, we'll perform an exercise that triggers your fight-or-flight reflex. It's an exercise that is sometimes uncomfortable, and always revealing.Benoist's Monkey Mind vs. Observing Mind

In Addicted to the Monkey Mind: Change the Programming that Sabotages Your Life, author JF Benoist explains the concept of the Monkey Mind.

The "Monkey Mind" gets its name "because it is less mature and evolved than the other aspects of our mind and thought processes. It's quick to react to something it doesn't agree with, as well as blame something or someone else for our problems."[6]

The Monkey Mind manufactures angst and anxiety. To quiet the Monkey Mind, Benoist teaches, you must develop the Observing Mind. While the Monkey Mind is like a child throwing a tantrum, the Observing Mind "does not look to other people or situations as the source of our troubles. Instead, it offers an objective perspective uninhibited by our judgmental programming."[7]

Monkey Shines

Let's examine the role our Monkey Mind plays when we're attacked by stalkers, harassers and Internet trolls.

Any external stimulus – a tweet, an Instagram comment, an in-person slight – can spring the Monkey Mind into action, where it "dominates our thoughts with stories related to our self-defeating core beliefs."[8]

Exploring how those core beliefs developed in our childhood is a key part of Benoist's book. For the purposes of this chapter's exercise, though, we'll focus on the core beliefs themselves and not their origin.

We'll start by seeing how our protagonists would complete an Illogical Conclusions exercise, then apply the steps of that exercise to our own situation.

Karen the Karen

Over the past few months, Karen (Chapter 1) has gone to great lengths to avoid seeing the Internet mockery of her in-store outburst. When she uses YouTube, for example, she accesses the site using an "Incognito" browser so the site doesn't give regional "comedy" recommendations that might include the video.

Today, though, she has decided to face the fear.

Karen takes a deep breath and prepares to open the original Instagram video from the day of the confrontation. Her hands tremble as her thumbs key in the Instagram user's handle into the search bar. Her familiar fight-or-flight instinct kicks in once again, sending adrenaline through her body. Her pupils dilate and register the visual imprint she's been actively avoiding for months.

As the video plays, Karen scrolls down to the top-rated comment:

Gee, a real Women in Leadership instructional video right here. Karen the Karen! Give a literal "Karen" a ten cent raise above minimum wage and a "manager" nametag and watch the power trip.

Karen exhales audibly. She picks up her journal and

completes the Illogical Conclusions exercise.

Using the source material, write out the attack verbatim.

Gee, a real Women in Leadership instructional video here. Karen the Karen! Give a literal "Karen" a ten cent raise above minimum wage and a "manager" nametag and watch the power trip.

In a sentence or two, what does your Monkey Mind interpret this attack to say about you?

That what happened that day was because I was on a power trip, throwing my weight around to feel important.

Is the above statement true?

No! I hate confrontation and reminding customers to wear masks was by far the worst part of my job. I went out of my way every day to be good to customers and make them feel welcome.

What aspect of your self-worth felt threatened by the attack?

*The idea that I'm a b*tch. That's not what was said, but I feel like it's implied.*

Is the worst/most harsh judgment in the answer above true?

No. Anybody who knows me knows that.

Sometimes a social media comment or post includes multiple attacks and requires further unpacking. In this case, Karen knew she needed to compare the job-shaming aspect to her core beliefs about her career. She repeated the steps above.

In a sentence or two, what does your Monkey Mind

interpret this attack to say about you?

That I'm essentially a minimum-wage peon that doesn't deserve respect. That I was just handed a manager title on a whim.

Is the above statement true?

No! I worked at that location for nearly a decade, and I've worked in customer service and retail for more than 20 years. I deserved the role I had – and I wasn't just a front-line manager anyway.

What aspect of your self-worth felt threatened by the attack?

The idea that I'm some entry-level flunky. Not that there's anything wrong with being on the lowest rung at the store. But I'm not.

Is the worst/most harsh judgment in answer above true?

No. I am actually quite proud of my experience in retail sales and customer service.

By addressing the verbatim attacks head-on, Karen was able to identify the difference between what was ***actually said*** and how her Monkey Mind ***interpreted*** the Instagram commenter's attack. By using her Observing Mind, Karen saw that the attacks on her self-worth were not valid. Defending herself in her own words – and spelling them out by hand – allowed Karen to identify illogical conclusions, and at the same time allowed her to release dread and anxiety.

Lisa the Corona Killer

For Lisa (Chapter 2), posting even the most innocuous pictures and messages to a social media account seems to be an invitation to her trolls.

Reading this chapter along with us, Lisa opens up her Instagram app and scrolls down to a picture of her Thanksgiving dinner table, where she hosted family and friends this year.

The first negative comment:

Nice spread! If you look closely, you see the ghost of Scott, warning the other guests that Lisa the Corona Killer is about to send them to the grave too.

Writing in her journal, Lisa completes the Illogical Conclusions exercise:

Using the source material, write out the attack verbatim.

Nice spread! If you look closely, you see the ghost of Scott, warning the other guests that Lisa the Corona Killer is about to send them to the grave too.

In a sentence or two, what does your Monkey Mind interpret this attack to say about you?

That I killed Scott. That I'd do the same to my friends and family and anyone, really.

Is the above statement true?

No. I would never have done any harm to Scott or anyone I care about.

What aspect of your self-worth felt threatened by the attack?

The idea that my political career is the most important thing to me, and that I'm selfish above all else. That's not what was said here, but that's what I feel is implied.

Is the worst/most harsh judgment in the answer above true?

No. I've given countless hours to my church, organizations in my community, and friends and family out of love. Not selfishness.

Accusations of murderous intentions can range from serious to ludicrous. When the charges are shouted from the darkness of the Instagram Court of Comments, they are frightening. Only by exposing them to the light, like Lisa did here, can she see their flimsiness in plain sight.

Alyssa Up for Grabs

Like Karen and Lisa, Alyssa's visual images elicit online reactions too. In Alyssa's case, though, the pictures were posted without her knowledge or consent.

Reading this chapter along with us, Alyssa visits the image-hosting website that she avoided for months. She enters "Alyssa" in the search bar, and the results show dozens of results "exposing" women who share her first name. She recognizes the fake name she believes James used to post her pictures. She taps the link, and momentarily holds her breath.

There's the post.

The description:

Hey guys – this chick Alyssa H. has been on a Tinder roll lately. I hooked up with her one night then found out my buddy hooked up with her a few days later. Anyway, here's a few pics she sent me. I've also seen these pics over on this awesome new page called Anonymous Revenge Posting Site. Give this girl what she really wants and make her famous!

The familiar feelings of rage and powerlessness seem to be welling up directly in Alyssa's tear ducts. She lets herself cry for a moment, welcoming the feelings instead of burying them. Then she steadies herself and begins writing in her journal.

Using the source material, write out the attack verbatim.

Hey guys – this chick Alyssa H. has been on a Tinder roll lately. I hooked up with her one night then found out my buddy hooked up with her a few days later. Anyway, here's a few pics she sent me. I've also seen these pics over on this awesome new page called Anonymous Revenge Posting Site. Give this girl what she really wants and make her famous!

In a sentence or two, what does your Monkey Mind interpret this attack to say about you?

*That I'm a complete sl*t that goes around hooking up with a different guy every week. That I'm desperate for male attention so I send pictures of myself around to anyone who is interested.*

Is the above statement true?

No. I have never even used a dating app and if I did, I'd never send those kinds of pictures before meeting a guy.

What aspect of your self-worth felt threatened by the attack?

The idea that I don't value any sort of privacy for myself. The idea that I am so desperate that I send guys pictures of myself for attention. Desperate AND stupid.

Is the worst/most harsh judgment in answer above true?

Absolutely not. James was one of the only guys I've ever sent those kinds of pictures to. And I'm not desperate at all. And I'm not so dumb as to send pictures of myself to men I've never met.

Observe that in all three examples, our protagonists reacted to what they thought was implied by the online comments, not necessarily the comments themselves. It's impossible for us to read the minds of even our closest friends and family members – we certainly cannot deduce the intentions of anonymous online trolls.

Journal

Now's the time to face the negative, hurtful and/or shame-inducing material you've likely been both avoiding *and* replaying in your mind.

From memory, or using the original source material, write down a statement from your stalker/harasser/Internet troll that triggered you to react emotionally.

In a sentence or two, what does your Monkey Mind interpret this attack to say about you?

Is the above statement true?

What aspect of your self-worth felt threatened by the attack?

Is the worst/most harsh judgment in answer above true?

Orientation continues

In this chapter, you've allowed yourself to experience the benefits of exposure therapy, facing the attacks against you head-on.

You now have a process to use the next time your stalkers, harassers and Internet trolls attack. The Illogical Conclusions exercise takes those external attacks and stacks them up against your internal beliefs. Doing so underscores how off-base the attacks really are.

But what about your own internal wants that you're projecting outward? For example, we saw in this chapter how Alyssa was concerned about her co-workers disapproving of what they might see in her Google search results.

What are the major “wants” we’re trying to satiate as we deal with the attacks upon us? We’ll learn about each in the next chapter.

CHAPTER 8: ORIENT: THE MIRAGE OF CONTROL, SECURITY AND APPROVAL

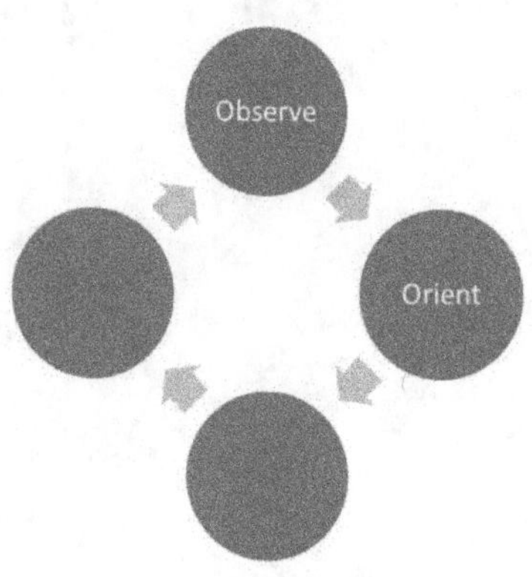

In Chapter 7, we used the specific word-for-word attacks from our stalkers, harassers, and Internet trolls to see how they challenged our core beliefs. Those core beliefs influence how we both assess and defend our self-worth.

Picture a forest. If the last chapter helped us dig deeper and explore the roots of our anxieties, this chapter will take an aerial view for a bigger picture. We'll observe that the attacks on us prey upon our three main human wants.

At the end of this chapter, you will be able to identify which of your three human wants are being exploited by your stalker, harasser or Internet troll. And you will have developed skills on how to begin the lifelong process of letting go of – or "releasing" – your previously unquenchable thirst to satiate those needs.

Basic human wants

In The Sedona Method, Hale Dwoskin explains the four basic human wants: control, security, approval, and separation. For our specific purposes in dealing with the effects of a stalker/harasser/Internet troll, we'll focus on the first three (control, security, and approval) and omit the fourth (separation.)[9]

Dwoskin explains: "Interestingly, each want includes an opposite or opposing force. So, not only does wanting create a sense of lack for us, we also experience varying degrees of conflict between wanting to control and to be controlled, wanting approval and disapproval, wanting security and insecurity .... Furthermore, every situation we find ourselves in triggers these opposing forces to a greater or lesser extent in our conscious awareness."[10]

Each of our protagonists experienced attacks on their basic human wants. Let's explore how.

Tyler and the Illusion of Control

In Chapter 4, we saw how deeply Tyler was affected by lust. Not lust in a carnal or sensual sense, but in the overwhelming desire for **more**. It might seem like what Tyler was craving **more** of was attention. Social media was his method to obtain that attention, and he even created a second Twitter account in this lust for **more**.

But it wasn't attention Tyler was seeking – it was control.

Dwoskin notes that wanting control "feels hard and pushy,

like: 'It has to be my way.' When we **want** to control we feel **out of control** and like we need to **take action** to get it back."[11] (Emphasis added.)

Attention is like currency – it comes and goes, ebbs and flows. Tyler earned attention and external validation based upon his Twitter activity. But attention was simply the currency that he used to pay his control deficit.

How did he get here?

Recall that Tyler's arrival in town was met with insta-snark from Dan Andrews. In his college communications classes, Tyler learned public relations mantras like, "Control the narrative," and "Get out in front of the story."

Tyler perceived Dan Andrews as controlling Tyler's own narrative, and Tyler was determined to get out in front of the Twitter-told story.

The path forward

In Chapter 4, Tyler acknowledged that his present situation is unmanageable. The burden of managing multiple sock-puppet Twitter accounts, and the fear of getting found out, has become unbearable.

Reading this chapter along with us, Tyler gets out his journal and answers the following.

What's a specific instance in which you felt a lack of control?

The first time I saw myself tagged in a tweet from Dan Andrews. When he called me "Tyler the Toady."

What's your **now** feeling about that moment?

I'm still dismayed that he chose to take a shot at me. But I'm proud I fought back, and didn't let those allegations go unchallenged.

What feels good about **lacking** control in this situation?

The lacking doesn't feel good at first, but I feel like I'm winning the battle every week by taking control back and that feels good. Dan's ridiculous allegations do not go unchallenged, and I know that I'm distracting him from attacking other people.

Does your response to your stalker/harasser/Internet troll involve wanting control, approval or security?

I am definitely wanting control, for the reasons above. And on some level I am seeking approval of all the people watching. I want them to see how clever my responses are, and I love seeing them respond favorably to my tweets. And on some level, security plays a role too. The better the @DanAndys responses to Dan are, the more I feel like it would be harder for my bosses to penalize me for Dan's attacks on me.

How has trying to control/influence your stalker/harasser/Internet troll affected your life?

It has certainly taken up more time than I thought at first. And I've pretty much become addicted to Twitter, if I wasn't already. When I get notifications of a new follow or reply, I feel a rush of dopamine as I open the app and see who or what it is.

Consider, in this moment, that you have released your desire to control or influence your stalker/harasser/Internet troll. You have accepted that you are in control **only** of how **you** handle **your own** thoughts, feelings, and choices of your actions. How does that feel?

Just thinking about it feels like some weight is off my shoulders. I usually feel like I'm on the clock or "on call" and need to respond to Dan's tweets every day, as if that will somehow get him to throw in the towel on his obsessive tweeting.

Could you let go of your desire to control or influence your Internet troll?

I could. A little bit. It is hard, though.

What **does** it feel like to release some amount of that desire to control?

It feels a little better. I feel a little bit more at peace.

In his shoes

Tyler is just beginning to learn the releasing process, and we observe that he experiencing the benefits incrementally.

We cannot read others minds', but we can relate to the thoughts and feelings of people experiencing the same type of stalking/harassing/Internet trolling that we have experienced.

Using your Observing Mind (Chapter 7), consider:

Is it possible Tyler is exaggerating the importance of Dan's tweets?

Does it seem like Tyler might actually enjoy the lack of control over Dan's tweets, and the chaos they create?

Does it appear that Tyler has spun a web of rationalizations for his own irrational behavior?

Listen to yourself

When we're wanting to control our stalker/harasser/ Internet troll, our self-talk sounds like this:

"I need to keep an eye out for what they're saying about me."

"I need my friends to keep their ears open for anything they hear about what he might do next."

"I haven't checked his <Twitter/Instagram/Facebook/forums>

in a while. Better check them now to see what he's up to."

"If she says <imaginary attack>, I'm going to reply immediately with <imaginary response.>"

Keith and the Safety Dance

In Chapter 5, we watched how Keith's Anger affected how he handled stalking from his former acquaintance Chris. Chris' stalking was obsessive, from the "Mobile Payment News Service" website creation to mocking the deaths of Keith's mom and dad. It wasn't until Chris had a meaningful piece of "news" – the online case records for Keith's DWI – that Keith's reactive Anger was dialed up to an unbearable level.

In The Sedona Method, Dwoskin writes that when we are wanting security, "(w)e see everyone, at least on a subtle level, as an enemy... We may avoid taking risks, even if that means giving up success.... We may walk around expecting the next disaster."[12]

Keith's sense of **impending disaster** was oppressive. He knew that few things are as dangerous as a person with nothing left to lose. Chris had already abandoned his own child, stole from his own mother, and was in deep debt to state officials.

"What's keeping him from violently attacking me?" Keith asks himself.

The path forward

Keith gets out his journal and answers the following questions.

What's a specific instance in which you felt like your stalker's actions threatened your security?

The first tweets from Chris years ago included my employer, and he even created fake profiles on our city's newspaper website to pretend to be me. That profile included my company's name in the profile picture. Then of course more recently, he tweeted his hate-blog post about my DWI arrest along with the court case entries.

What's your **now** feeling about that moment?

It still makes me mad. Chris finally had something to criticize me for after my DWI, and of course he pounced on it.

What feels good about having your security **threatened** by this type of stalking/harassment?

I never really thought about it feeling "good," but reflecting on it now, it gave me an opportunity talk to my company's global security team, along with the company's social media lead and my direct manager. Until then I had no real reason to explain the insanity I was facing with Chris' stalking.

Does your response to your stalker/harasser/Internet troll involve wanting control, approval or security?

There's an approval sense, for sure. It feels good to know that my manager and my company's HR department have my back. It felt good to hear their reaction to the most obsessive actions of Chris, like celebrating my parents' death. There was a sense of control involved too, since the global security team let me know that Chris was now on their watch list, and that campus security was aware of his threatening behavior. And the security aspect itself is pretty clear in that I feel better knowing that my job isn't threatened by some loose cannon taking aim at me and my company.

How has feeling a lack or want of security involving your stalker/harasser/Internet troll affected your life?

I've held back from posting to social media about some of the career accomplishments I'm most proud of. I feel like Chris would just repost them to his hate blog and use it as another excuse to attack me and my company.

Consider, in this moment, that you have released your want of security, or conversely, released your desire to feel like you're always in danger. You no longer view every daily action through the filter of being under attack. How do you feel?

I feel more relieved just reading those words. I know I overprepare for the next online attack and let it dominate my thoughts throughout the day.

Could you let go of your desire to feel secure, or conversely, your desire to feel like you're always in danger?

Maybe. In some ways, it feels like I'm in a foxhole, always defending myself against Chris' attacks. And after all this time, the good thing is that now I feel like my co-workers and at least a couple higher-ups in the company are in that foxhole with me. So being under attack is a familiar and somewhat comfortable feeling. But I also want to escape from under that constant cloud.

What **does** it feel like as you begin releasing that desire for security?

It feels freeing. Like I can walk out of my house or my office and not be paranoid that I have to check my phone for the latest online attack.

In his shoes

One's personal safety, and the safety of loved ones, is a primary concern when dealing with stalkers/harassers/ Internet trolls.[13] Feeling as if our security is threatened can have a paralyzing effect on our social and professional lives.

Using your Observing Mind (Chapter 7), consider:

Is it possible Keith allotted undue attention to Chris' hate blog?

Might Keith have been using the "foxhole" mentality to avoid taking action in other areas of his life?

How might Keith's view of the stalking/harassment have changed if Keith focused exclusively on his own choices (e.g., no more drinking and driving, continued personal growth, professional advancement) and ignored Chris' hateful obsession?

Listen to yourself

When we're wanting security, our self-talk might sound like this:

"It's coming. I can just feel it."

"She's been too quiet lately. She's preparing her next series of posts."

"I can't stick my neck out too far. Just keep a low profile and don't invite any more attacks."

Gabby and the Thirst for Approval

In Chapter 6, we witnessed the role of Gabby's pride in the face of incessant trolling from Kelley Lynn. Gabby's #BossBabe text thread cheered every one of Gabby's petty reactions and overreactions as if they were watching a sporting event – they even appropriated terms like "spiking the football" and "victory lap" to describe those moments.

Of course, unlike in a real sporting activity, there were no objective points being scored and there was no meaningful record kept. There ***was*** a never-ending race being run, though. It was a marathon race for Gabby, at which the only sustenance provided was approval.

Gabby's #BossBabe friends were set up alongside the social media marathon course, handing out miniature cups of approval water. And each cup offered a few ounces of sustenance. But the tiny serving sizes would never quench Gabby's thirst for approval – in fact, she didn't realize the ultimate finish line was really approval from Kelley Lynn herself.

How did she get here?

As a young woman in male-dominated college classes, Gabby grew accustomed to standing out and being praised. But her appointment to lead the transit authority was a headlong dive into the shark-infested waters of local politics. It didn't matter to Kelley that Gabby was supremely qualified for the transit role. Gabby was merely a proxy of the new administration, and a seemingly soft target for Kelley's attacks.

The path forward

Despite Gabby's prideful and boastful Twitter persona, the eternal battle against Kelley is taking its toll. As a socially intelligent woman, Gabby senses that her friends are getting a bit tired of the overplayed story and they seem incrementally less enthused about being dragged into the daily drama.

Gabby gets out her journal and answers the following questions:

What's a specific instance in which you felt like you weren't getting the approval you deserved?

The first tweet from Kelley Lynn about my "on the job training."

What's your **now** feeling about that moment?

I'm glad I rallied the troops. It felt good to know there was a group of people who cheered for me and who had my back.

What feels good about **lacking** approval in these Twitter battles?

When I'm disrespected by Kelley, I know my #BossBabe posse will take up the fight. And then I'm tallying yet another win over Kelley.

Does your response to your stalker/harasser/Internet troll involve wanting control, approval or security?

I definitely am wanting control, because I'm not going to let Kelley control the narrative about my job performance. That's my story to tell, not hers. And security is part of that too – especially my job security. The mayor needs to see and understand that I am being attacked by his enemies, and he needs to stand by my side no matter what. And as I mentioned above, I do enjoy the approval of my #BossBabe text thread. Most days their texts are the only source of strength I can find.

Could you let go of your desire to earn approval – or disapproval – from your instigating behavior?

I don't know. It's addictive! The day-to-day aspects of the transit authority role can be pretty measured and boring. This battle fuels my sense of purpose. And it feels so good to take one little action, like wearing my red lipstick on camera, and getting that immediate reaction from Kelley Lynn.

How has trying to get approval – or disapproval – from Kelley and your #BossBabe text thread affected your life?

It's exhausting. While it has made my job more interesting in some ways, it has also undermined the satisfaction I used to get from a job well done. Now it's not about succeeding or wrapping up a project for its own sake – I feel like every victory needs to be documented and celebrated for show.

Consider, in this moment, that you have released your desire to gain approval – or disapproval – from Kelley or your #BossBabe thread. You have accepted that you are the most relevant, competent and meaningful judge of your performance. Do you feel more in control and at peace?

Yes. I AM the best judge of my performance. But I also really want everybody else to know that I know that too!

What **would** it feel like to release some amount of that desire to gain approval?

It would feel like less striving. It's exhausting attending all the social events I do, mostly to troll Kelley. And I would start to put myself and my job first, rather than making Kelley the center of my attention and intentions.

What **does** it feel like as you begin releasing that desire to gain approval?

It feels like a relief. And as a bonus I want to know if my #BossBabe friends are really my friends, or if they're just swept up in the drama along with me.

In her shoes

People with a strong sense of social media pride sit upon a razor's edge of external validation; when they sense a stalker/harasser/Internet troll withholding approval, the prideful may go out of their way to create **even more** disapproval.

Using your Observing Mind (Chapter 7), consider:

Is Gabby exaggerating the importance of Kelley Lynn's tweets?

Does Gabby seem to enjoy the lack of approval she receives from Kelley? What actions tell you so?

How might Gabby feel if Kelley suddenly deactivated her Twitter account?

How might Gabby feel if Kelley had a change of heart about Gabby and the mayor's administration, and stopped trolling Gabby?

Does Gabby's #BossBabe text thread give honest feedback on Gabby's actions, or does it reflexively encourage and enable Gabby's approval-seeking behavior? Are they the type of women that would enable other self-destructive behaviors?

Listen to yourself

When we're wanting approval or disapproval in the face of stalkers/harassers/Internet trolls, our self-talk might sound like this:

"My friends are going to LOVE this response."

"It's late at night, so I'll reply to that tweet/comment/post when people are awake and can see it. I don't want anyone to miss it!"

"Haha! She's going to HATE this post. How can I make it just a little bit meaner?"

Journal

It's time to identify how your three human wants of control, security and approval are being exploited by your stalker, harasser or Internet troll. Using your journal, answer the following questions.

What's a specific instance in which you felt like the attack on you left you wanting control, security or approval?

*What's your **now** feeling about that moment?*

*What feels good about **lacking** control, security or approval in these situations?*

Does your response to your stalker/harasser/Internet troll's attack involve wanting control, security or approval?

How has feeling a lack or want of control, security or approval in your stalker/harasser/Internet troll situation affected your life?

*What **would** it feel like to release some amount of that desire for control, security or approval?*

*What **does** it feel like as you begin releasing your desire for control, security or approval?*

Orient, Expressed

You're now able to identify which of your three major wants are preyed upon by your stalker/harasser/Internet troll. And you have a process by which you can begin letting go – or "releasing" – those wants as they arise in your mind.

You'll notice yourself applying this knowledge to the attacks you witness on social media platforms daily. And you'll recognize when others' reflexive retorts are centered around their own **wants** of control, security, and approval.

Is enough enough?

"Have you punished yourself enough?" That's a question Hale Dwoskin asks in The Sedona Method.

The answer, to the Observing Mind, is always, "Yes." But your ever-present Monkey Mind may resist moving on. In the next chapter, we'll explore why.

CHAPTER 9: DECIDE: ARE YOU REALLY READY TO LET GO OF THE PAINFUL PAST?

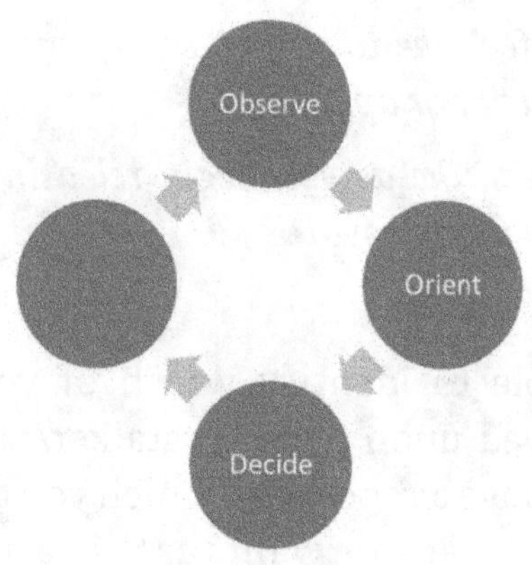

Pain is my shepherd; I shall not feel joy.

2 He maketh me to lie down and stay burrowed in bed: he leadeth me to drink and drug and numb the anxiety away.

3 He restoreth my youthful insecurities: he leadeth me in the paths of shame for shame's sake.

4 Yea, though I can see the mountaintop of courage and acceptance, I will achieve no peace: for thou art with me; thy resentment and regret, they comfort me.

5 Thou preparest a table before me in the presence of mine enemies: thou anointest my mind with revenge; my rage runneth over.

[6] Surely stress and anxiety shall follow me all the days of my life: and I will dwell in the house of Pain forever.

- Not Psalm 23

Your painful past is familiar. Your painful past is comforting.

Apathy wraps you in the warm weighted blanket of stillness and sloth. When you're supine on the couch, lamenting your luck and feeling sorry for yourself, the sofa cushions cradle your body just right. The television remote fits warmly in your grip like it was custom-made for your hand. There's no need to get up. What's the use?

Grief gives you a permanent pass to isolate. That group of friends who keeps inviting you to events doesn't really care about you, anyway. They won't miss you if you just stay home. Everyone else has moved on with their lives. Besides, you need time to mourn. Don't rush it. Stay where you are.

Fear gives you firm boundaries to protect what's left of your feelings from getting bruised. Like a mouse nestled between flophouse floorboards, you squeeze down and in between your mind's rigid constraints to keep yourself safe. Don't stick your neck out too far, or wander too far from the safe space, or else you'll get clawed by the stalking cat.

Lust makes you feel alive. After all, if you're getting more, you cannot be stuck with less. If you're growing, you're not dying. If you're sticking it to someone else, you're affecting your external world. You can see the proof.

Anger is the fuel that drives progress. Isn't that how nations are born and civilizations are created? 'We must stop demonizing anger,' you rationalize as you set out to settle the score. You're not complacent and you're not paralyzed by fear – you're TAKING ACTION.

Pride is the self-justified feeling that you are entitled to proper respect. You'll make sure of it. You love your critics and detractors, you claim. If Instagram influencers and pop music lyrics have taught you anything about success, it's that 'haters' are the fuel that drives you forward.

Are you ready to leave these emotions behind?

If you purchased this guide, your answer to the above is probably a reflexive "yes."

But often, these low-frequency emotions are integral to who you identify as "you" today.

Cool story, bro

Stalking stories are captivating. The tales are colorful, yet the characters themselves are purely black and white.

There's you, the protagonist, doing your best to traverse the ups and downs of life. Then from out of the shadows, the villain emerges. Driven by dark desires and filled with cruel intentions, this malevolent character unleashes an attack.

"Can you believe it?" your facial expression shouts to your audience as you tick through the beats of this story you know by heart.

In The Sedona Method, Hale Dwoskin explains why we cling to our traumatic experiences. A man named Kenneth was a direct witness to the terrorist attacks in New York City on Sept. 11, 2001 and confessed to Dwoskin that he was unwilling to let go of his post-attack anxiety. Dwoskin writes:

> It wasn't until (Kenneth) was able to recognize how he was subtly proud of having been in such a unique situation, and developing such a great story about it, that he was able to let go completely. Once he did see the pride and released it, the anxiety that he'd been experiencing vanished and did not reoccur.[14]

Dr. Joe Dispenza, author of Breaking the Habit of Being Yourself, summarized it as such:

> We've all had situations in our life where we've been betrayed, traumatized, manipulated, or abused in one way or another. When something like this occurs,

> our internal alarm systems switch on, & in doing so, because the event is so threatening or painful, the brain freezes the frame & takes a snapshot of the external event. We call this a long-term memory. The side effect is the survival emotions are triggered. Because those chemicals are so unpleasant, we do whatever we can to avoid them. In trying to avoid them, we keep reliving & revisiting the memory of the event over & over again, & now we're stuck in a loop of thinking & feeling the very emotions that we don't want to feel.
>
> As a result, our entire perception of the world becomes based on that memory. This is what keeps the body connected to the past. By holding on to some problem & keeping your attention on the past event or person who you feel is responsible for your pain, you are allowing that person or event to hold you emotionally hostage. That means you're giving away your energy, your power to create, & your life force to something outside of you.[15]

Our stalkers, harassers and Internet trolls wish to be inextricably linked to us. They yearn to live like a cancerous tumor inside our bodies and our minds.

Can you allow yourself to cut them out?

Journal

What would your life look like without feeling trapped under the cloud of your stalker/harasser/Internet troll?

Would you finally feel comfortable posting pictures of you with your friends and family again?

Are there places you've been avoiding because you fear running into acquaintances who've seen the attacks on you?

Would you finally start that project you've been putting off "until all this blows over"?

Take some time to capture these thoughts in your journal.

Meditate on how it feels to be free from your stalker/harasser/Internet troll.

The "D" in OODA Loop is Decide. If you have decided to move on from the painful past, advance to the next chapter, move into Action.

CHAPTER 10: ACT: INTRODUCING CHRIS – COWARDICE VS. COURAGE

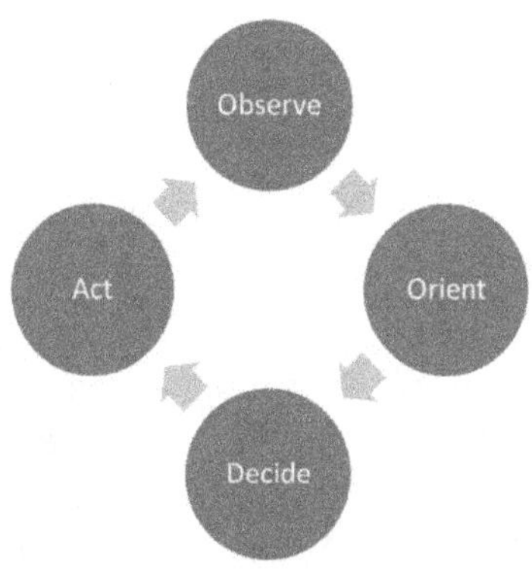

In chapters 1 through 6, we observed how varying methods of stalking, harassment and Internet trolling affected the lives of six people. From a third-person omniscient view, we observed how the actions of an antagonist or group of antagonists was eliciting a negative emotional response from our protagonists.

In Chapter 7, you made it personal. You learned how the words of **your own** antagonist(s) trigger your Monkey Mind to jump to illogical conclusions about yourself. Accordingly, you saw how activating your Observing Mind can short-circuit self-defeating mental pathways.

In Chapter 8, we saw how our desires for control, security

and approval are in fact unquenchable thirsts, and we learned techniques to begin releasing on those wants.

In Chapter 9, we affirmed our **decision** to move forward and take action.

In this chapter, we'll acknowledge for the first time the mutual antagonist in our lives, the person whose actions brought us together at this very moment – CHRIS.

The name CHRIS symbolizes our stalker/harasser/Internet troll's five key characteristics/traits:

Cowardice

Heaviness

Resentment

Isolation

Selfishness

Since it can apply to a man or a woman, **CHRIS** will be the working nickname collectively representing our stalkers/ harassers/Internet trolls. As you read the following chapters, you may find it expeditious to use an acronym for **S**talkers/**H**arassers/**I**nternet **T**rolls. The acronym can be used interchangeably with CHRIS.

Together we'll explore the five characteristics of CHRIS, and how you can avoid the trap of emulating those traits yourself. Since we cannot control the actions of **others**, only ourselves, we'll explore the five personality traits, skills and habits **you** must develop and practice to slay and transcend your own stalkers/harassers/Internet trolls.

You might have heard the axiom that carrying resentment is like swallowing poison and expecting the other person to die. In the coming chapters, we'll reference each of CHRIS' traits as a dose of poison. Trying to match CHRIS with his own hate traits would be like swallowing shots of each of his five toxic cocktails. Instead, you'll put into practice the antidote of each.

Let's begin.

CHRIS trait: Cowardice

In most cases, CHRIS is terrified of speaking to you face to face. Even if CHRIS mustered up the courage to speak to you in person, they'd have a hard time keeping up the façade of their fearless, uber-confident social media voice.

This trait is timeless. With each iteration of communication technology, cowards have found a way to use it anonymously. They have been hiding their identities as they sent snail-mail letters (1970s), made phone calls from pay phones (1980s), and dialed *67 to block caller ID (1990s). The Internet and social media have simply made it easier for anonymous CHRISes to cover their tracks.

In chapters one through six, some of our protagonists dealt with truly anonymous attacks. Lisa, for example, received the bulk of her harassment and trolling from anonymous Twitter accounts. The anonymity from those attacking Lisa might be expected, as few people would want their real names attached to the harassment of a widow.

You may be experiencing a situation, like Alyssa and Keith, where your CHRIS' identity is known – but he/she uses an anonymous account for deniability. Keith's stalker/harasser/Internet troll posts to the "Mobile Payment News Service" blog with the default author label "admin," and Alyssa's ex-boyfriend created a generic username to post her photos and create the "Anonymous Revenge Posting Site."

The paradox, of course, is that these CHRISes seeks to "expose" while they lurk in the shadow of an Internet pseudonym.

The Trap: Tit-for-tat

Recall Tyler, the newspaper reporter being trolled by local gadfly Dan Andrews (Chapter 4.) Tyler succumbed to the temptation of trolling Dan back, and the @DanAndys Twitter account was born. Tyler even created additional bogus accounts to intensify his retributive trolling.

The difference between the trolls? Dan Andrews had the

courage to put his name on his opinions. "@DanAndys" didn't.

"Fighting fire with fire" by creating anonymous accounts is a fool's errand. It's the social media version of a sugar high – the immediate rush is brief and unsustainable. Tyler discovered that maintaining his own troll accounts was exhausting, and the fear of being identified as their author weighed on him daily.

The antidote: Courage

Once you have made your decision to not replicate CHRIS' cowardice though anonymous clapbacks, the next step is demonstrating courage.

Full recovery from stalking/harassment/Internet trolling attacks requires authenticity and openness. Those principles can be hard to maintain in the wake of an embarrassing online attack.

Demonstrating courage has two components: owning up and showing up.

Owning up

Chances are, you've told your stalking/harassment/Internet trolling story so many times that in its current version, you are the perfect protagonist. You might portray yourself as entirely blameless and depict the antagonist (CHRIS) as an illogical madman/madwoman, who launched his or her attack unprovoked.

But is that really true?

There is a fine line between "victim blaming" and accountability, and for those of us who have been attacked, it can be an imposing mental hurdle. It is, however, possible to avoid CHRIS' gaslighting while still taking ownership of any activities and behaviors that invited his/her stalking/harassment/Internet trolling.

Keith immediately disregarded Chris' meandering conspiracy-theory writings, and never linked to Chris' blog. Chris viewed this a personal insult, which sparked the idea of creating an anti-Keith hate site.

Gabby's carefully-curated social media presence was designed to inflame Kelley Lynn – all the way down to her frequent swipes against "over the hill" consultants.

We do not control the actions of others, but some of us orchestrate situations in which we influence and bait others.

Journal –10.1

Did you play a role in encouraging, amplifying or extending an online attack against you? How so? If so, were your actions a result of your own ego, pride, or self-satisfaction?[16]

Showing up

CHRIS wants you in a box. Constricted, contained, voiceless.

We'll cover isolation in detail in Chapter 13. For now, we'll focus on showing up in physical and virtual places.

The attack is out there – on Twitter, Facebook, Instagram, a hate blog. "They've all seen it," you say to yourself.

CHRIS may even use surveillance tactics to intimidate you into shrinking. Dan Andrews monitored the new brewery's Instagram video stream to capture still shots of Tyler. Kelley Lynn reacted in real time to Gabby's social posts from community events.

Journal – 10.2

List any activities that CHRIS' surveillance has kept you from participating in, or the locations and events that the threat of surveillance has caused you to avoid. This might include resistance to maintaining a basic social media profile or staying away from community events you used to attend regularly.

CHAPTER 11: ACT: HEAVY VS. LIGHT

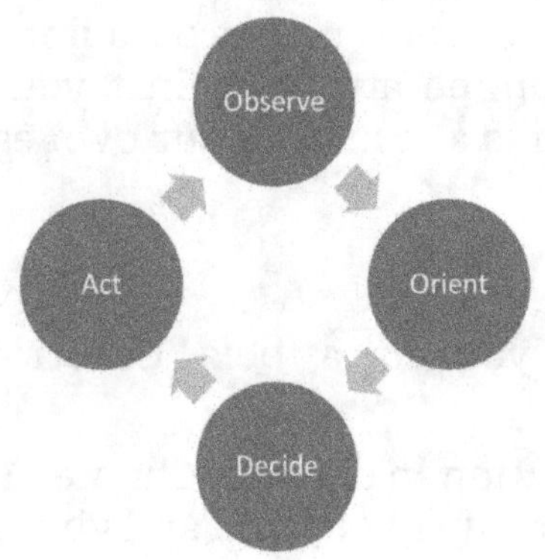

CHRIS trait: Heaviness

CHRIS is a bottom-feeder in word and deed. As such, it helps to visualize CHRIS at the bottom of the ocean, operating a giant anchor with a pulley attached. Your ship has been tethered to CHRIS' rope for as long as your conscious mind has been battling their stalking/harassment/Internet trolling tactics. CHRIS' mission is two-fold: to keep your ship from moving on, and at the same time trying to pull you underwater to his lonely depths.

The Trap: Staying tethered to heavy anchors

We saw in Chapters 1-6 that the antagonists were acting out based on their own heavy emotions. Alyssa's ex-boyfriend James (Chapter 3) was feeling grief from losing Alyssa; Kelley Lynn (Chapter 6) was still mourning the departure of her ex-boss, the corrupt mayor.

Even bottom-feeders need oxygen – and your attention is CHRIS' oxygen. The worst-case, doomsday scenarios for stalkers/harassers/Internet trolls is being ignored by their targets.

The antidote: Lightness – moving up the emotional scale

The only way to counter heavy emotions is by accessing lighter emotions.

We'll utilize two approaches to moving up the emotional scale.

Traditional Sedona Method Releasing

In Chapter 8, we practiced releasing our attachments to control, security and approval. The process of releasing is at the center of the Sedona Method approach and is the cornerstone of releasing each of the emotional levels we examined in Chapters 1-6.

At the core of the Sedona Method's release approach are four questions. After an emotion has been identified, ask yourself:

Can I welcome this feeling?

Can I let it go?

Would I let it go?

When?

Example: After reading Chapters 1-6, perhaps you have identified Fear as your "right now" feeling about your situation. Perhaps someone has attempted to shame you by posting embarrassing information, pictures or videos to a website or social media platform. Or perhaps someone is threatening to "expose" facts or rumors about your business or personal relationships.

Using the traditional Sedona Method technique, ask yourself:

Can I welcome this feeling of fear?

You cannot release a feeling you have not welcomed, and you cannot welcome a feeling you are resisting.

Welcoming the fear will feel unnatural at first, because you have likely been pushing back against it. Your tactics of resistance might have included avoidance, denial, or some combination of both.

Can I let it go?

Having welcomed the fear, you're now free to let it go. Sedona Method training sessions often include a "pencil grip" exercise; just as your hand can grip a pencil tightly, it just as easily can release the grip and let the pencil fall. If you're having difficulty releasing fear at this step, implement the pencil metaphor and envision yourself alternately gripping, then releasing, the feeling of fear.

Would I let it go?

In Chapter 7, we acknowledged our love/hate relationship with the painful emotions brought about by online attacks. If you are indeed ready to move on, restate your willingness here.

When?

One key advantage of the Sedona Method is its immediate application. It's a "now" process – unlike some other mindset approaches, the Sedona Method is not dependent on origin stories or long-term vision boards. You can begin releasing any emotion, including fear, at any moment. Will you make that moment **now**?

<u>Brian Begin/Fearless Man Method</u>

A second, alternate approach to releasing comes from Brian Begin, who created the Fearless Man training programs. Begin's approach is consistent with the foundational teachings of the traditional Sedona Method but focuses on beginning with the highest-level emotions – Courage, Acceptance and Peace – rather than starting at the bottom with Apathy.

Begin's modified approach was borne from working with students attempting to release the lowest-level emotions of Apathy, Grief and Fear. He observed that students learned to successfully release those emotions, but never seemed to achieve higher-level emotions.

In his words:

"(When) you're doing all the releasing down here (Apathy, Grief, Fear) this becomes your whole world. If the whole time I'm saying, 'Can I welcome Fear and let it go?' 'Can I welcome Grief and let it go?' 'Can I welcome Apathy and let it go?' ... But I never spend much time up here (highest-level emotions) your subconscious mind doesn't have a relationship to Courage, Acceptance, Peace."[17]

Begin's students read a list of "subtle emotions" associated with Courage, Acceptance, and Peace. In his words:

"Courage has a whole host of other emotions that go with it. There's a sense of adventure in courage, a sense of being alert, a sense of being alive ... If you look at these emotions and you say, 'Can I remember a time I ever felt alert and what did that feel like? And how good did that feel?' 'Where did I feel it in my body?' And you meditate on that for a second, even if it's only 1%, a tiny little bit of feeling, that's really important for good releasing."

Journal

See the list below of emotions associated with Courage, Acceptance and Peace.[18]

Courage	Acceptance	Peace
alert	gracious	boundless
alive	nothing to change	calm
cheerful	open	fulfilled
flexible	understanding	serenity
resilient	warm	whole

For each of the three levels, pick three of the associated words and meditate on how they feel **in this moment**.

Examples:

Courageousness may sound like this: "Can I allow myself to feel alert, alive and cheerful? How can I act on this today?"

Acceptance might sound like this: "Can I allow myself to feel gracious, nothing to change, and open? How can I act on this today?"

Peace might sound like, "Can I allow myself to feel boundless, calm and whole? How can I act on this today?"

After experiencing the feelings associated with these levels, write down the action you will take today to achieve congruence with that feeling. If you follow a structured morning routine, you might choose to add this step to the routine.

CHAPTER 12: ACT: RESENTMENT VS. GRATITUDE

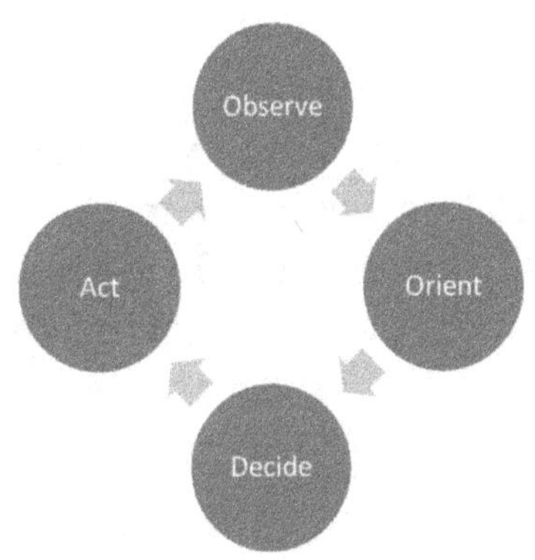

CHRIS trait: Resentment

"Hate comes from below," the cliché goes, and CHRIS punches up at you relentlessly. Your happiness is an affront to his sadness, your joy an insult to his pain.

Some of the most intense resentment comes from those who at one time saw you as an equal – a classmate, a work colleague, a lover.

Alyssa's ex-boyfriend resented her ability to move on after their romantic relationship ended.

Keith's acquaintance Chris resented the success of Keith's

blog, so Chris started an anti-Keith hate site.

Gabby's antagonist resented Gabby's youth and clean reputational slate. Gabby's political purity reminded Kelley Lynn of what public service was like before her former boss went to prison.

Of course, as Karen and Lisa learned, your stalker/harasser/ Internet troll has the capacity to resent you even if they've never met you

The Trap: Woe is me

Everyone is doing better than you, CHRIS wants you to believe. You're falling behind – in the chase for money, professional status, romantic affection, social media clout. Your peers are moving on and moving ahead without you, CHRIS insists.

Such was the case for Lisa in Chapter 2. Nine months after Scott's death, after the initial flood of sympathy texts to Lisa's phone dried to a trickle, what remained were the hateful social media messages from trolls. Meanwhile, Lisa's fellow public officials were filing new bills, holding fundraisers, prepping for the next election. They had moved on.

Luring you into the resentment trap serves CHRIS in several ways. It baits you into lashing out, sometimes publicly. It breeds animosity toward those in your social circle, the friends and family who could provide support during this challenging time. And it plants the seeds for two of CHRIS' other key traits, isolation and selfishness, which we'll explore in Chapters 13 and 14.

The Antidote: Gratitude

Two approaches to experiencing and expressing gratitude

are critical to recovering from CHRIS' stalking/ harassment/Internet trolling.

1.) Gratitude for what has happened and your present state

What if you allowed yourself to feel gratitude for the attacks upon you?

At first, the notion sounds absurd.

"How can a sane person feel gratitude for living in fear?" you ask.

Why should you be grateful for having your reputation dragged through the mud? For having your co-workers learn about the most intimate, private details of your personal life? It seems illogical.

But what if you were assured that by feeling gratitude for the attacks, you could actually make the pain of those attacks subside?

Academic institutes are expanding their studies of neuroplasticity – that is, "the ability of the nervous system to change its activity ... by reorganizing its structure, functions, or connections" – as results continue to show the effects that gratitude practices have on the brain. In short, the process of expressing gratitude demonstrates quantifiable effects on pain reduction and brain wave patterns consistent with an elevated emotional state.[19]

2.) Gratitude for future reality

We've been conditioned our entire lives to give thanks after we've registered an emotion or received a gift. But what if we gave thanks before anything external was presented to us?

This is the practice advanced by author and neuroscience

researcher Dr. Joe Dispenza throughout his teachings. He advises:

> Rather than waiting for an occasion to cause you to feel a certain way, create the feeling ahead of any experience in the physical realm; convince your body emotionally that a gratitude generating experience has already taken place. (p. 145)
>
> You may object that you can't know how it would feel, because you've never experienced what it's like to have those traits and to be that ideal self. My response is that your body can experience this before you have any physical evidence ahead of your senses ... the elevated emotions of gratitude, love, and so forth... will help you move into a state of being where you can feel as though the desired events have actually occurred. (...) Giving thanks allows you to emotionally condition your body to believe that what is producing your gratitude has already happened. By activating and coordinating your three brains, (you can) begin to move from thinking to being and once you are in a new state of being you are more prone to act and think equal to who you are being.[20]

Journal

Expressing gratitude daily is a cornerstone practice of 12-step recovery programs. The idea of a "daily" obligation, however, can seem overwhelming and onerous to beginners. As such, the exercises below ascend from easy to more challenging.

12.1 Who were the first 3 people to reach out to you after you were attacked? Text, email or call each of those people *today* and express your gratitude. (If one of the people is a family member or spouse with whom you live, have the conversation in person *today*.) Resist the temptation to include an action item (e.g., "Let's meet for coffee," "I owe you a beer") as your expression of gratitude should be entirely giving and not feel tied to a future obligation or reciprocity.

12.2 What is *one* positive consequence that came about from being attacked? Perhaps you finally sought help from a mental health professional after resisting the notion for years. Maybe you sought and developed a relationship with your Higher Power or were forced to take an honest look at your addiction to social media apps. List the first positive consequence that comes to mind. Can you add a second? A third?

12.3 Before going to bed each night, use your journal to capture three things *that happened that day* for which you are grateful. Putting specifics around events and actions rather than broad categories (e.g., "my friends," "my family") will raise your awareness of the opportunities and unexpected serendipities as they occur each day.

12.4 Following the Dispenza model of learning to experience the ecstasy of gratitude before an event has taken place: Imagine that you have been demonstrating Courage through the steps outlined in 10.1 and 10.2. Further, imagine that you are already accessing Courage, Acceptance and Peace daily, as you learned in Chapter 11 and have released the heavier emotions you were once facing.

What does that feel like? Can you allow yourself to give thanks for this new reality?

Don't be surprised if this proves challenging the first

few times you try. You're likely attempting to use your rational, task-oriented mind to solve an emotional puzzle. As Dispenza writes:

> Do not analyze; Do not try to figure out how it is going to happen. It is not your job to control the outcome. It is your task to create, and leave the details to a greater mind. As you see your future as the observer simply bless your life with your own energy...
>
> From a state of gratitude, be one with your destiny from a new state of mind and body. Give thanks for a new life ...[21]

CHAPTER 13: ACT: ISOLATION VS. SUPPORT

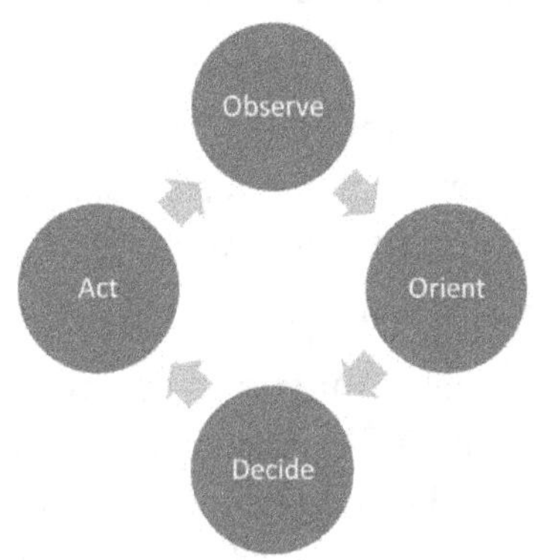

CHRIS trait: Isolation

It's impossible to read CHRIS' mind – but that hasn't stopped each of us from trying. Amid being attacked, most of us have spent hundreds if not thousands of waking hours deducing CHRIS' motivations.

Although we cannot be certain of CHRIS' thought patterns, we know that the trait that many of our stalkers/harassers/ Internet trolls seem to have in common is **isolation**.

Chances are, if CHRIS was living in abundance and surrounded by love – by friends and family with whom he shared a strong reciprocal bond – he wouldn't be attacking you.

Online spaces, particularly social media, provide a sense of community to people who might otherwise feel isolated. In many cases this is a net positive for society. For example, some seniors in assisted living communities use Facebook to stay in touch with family who can't make in-person visits. And teens who feel excluded from their school's "popular" cliques can find a sense of belonging through groups dedicated to hundreds of different niches.

Without a personal support network of their own, your CHRIS might manufacture a community online. Like a young child with invisible "friends," CHRIS builds shadow accounts and fake profiles to appear as though other people are cheering him/her on.

In many cases, the personal connection CHRIS craves most is the one with you. By keeping you anchored to him/her (Chapter 11), CHRIS believes they will never be alone.

The trap: I'll handle this myself, for now.

One of CHRIS' key strategies is to drive wedges between you and the people closest to you. It's a strategy that is as effective as it is devious.

By attacking you, CHRIS has laid a trap for you to feel awkward. He's affected your relationships with your friends, family, and co-workers. He's attempted to inject shame, guilt and embarrassment into those relationships, in the hope that you'll shrink and hide.

How do you know if CHRIS' trap has been successful? Your self-talk might sound like this:

"I'll handle this myself."

"I'll start going back to (family gatherings/church/happy hours/social events) after all this blows over."

This type of self-talk even shows up when friends reach out to check on you.

"I don't even want to get into that topic with them," you tell yourself. *"I'll talk to them about it later, when I'm in a better mental place."*

In the Observe section of this guide, we witnessed Karen (Chapter 1) and Lisa (Chapter 2) choosing isolation.

Karen walled herself off from close friends and family who were willing to discussing her situation face-to-face or on the phone. She was also stung the moment she opened her Facebook messages and saw no supportive messages from her online acquaintances.

Lisa felt the iciness of isolation when her friends and political colleagues moved on with their day-to-day lives and careers while she was still fending off troll messages.

Both chose to interpret silence from friends as tacit disapproval, ambivalence, or even worse – no cares given.

The antidote: Your personal support network

"Your network is your net worth," business gurus preach. The same can be said for personal support networks and our mental capital.

We learned about approval-seeking behaviors in Chapter 8, and that knowledge is foundational as we build our support networks. Two cornerstones to keep in mind:

- Our goal is ***not*** to establish an echo chamber comprised of sycophants who tell us what we want to hear.
- It ***is*** possible minimize our own approval-seeking behavior while still allowing ourselves to accept sincere praise for our good decisions, progress and

gains.

Journal

In his book Facing the Shadow, addiction guru Patrick Carnes outlines what he calls the "Important People Inventory." The idea, Carnes writes, is to "identify people who are important to you and describe how much they know about you."[22]

For the purpose of our journal, we'll modify the Carnes exercise to fit our own experiences with stalkers, harassers and Internet trolls.

Carnes instructs, "After filling in the following four lists with names, go back and rate each person on a scale of 1 to 5 based on how close you feel to that person. (A score of 1 means not close at all and a score of 5 represents a very close and trusting relationship.)"

13.1 To begin, list the people who know **everything** about your stalking/harassment/Internet trolling experience – including the substance of the attack and how it has affected you. Then assign a closeness rating.

Name	Closeness rating (1 to 5)

Next, list the people who know about **most** of your stalking/harassment/Internet trolling experience (i.e., people who know the basics of the attack(s) and how it has affected you) and assign a closeness rating.

Name	Closeness rating (1 to 5)

Next, list the people who know **a little** about your stalking/harassment/Internet trolling experience. For example, this might include people who heard second-hand you were in a "Facebook fight" or "got people stirred up." Assign each of these people a closeness rating.

Name	Closeness rating (1 to 5)

Finally, list the people who are important to you but who know **nothing** about your stalking/harassment/Internet trolling experience. Then assign each a closeness rating.

13.2 – Carnes' follow-up exercise from Facing the Shadow instructs us to reflect on our Important People Inventory. Once again, for the purpose of our journal, we'll modify this Carnes exercise to fit our own experiences with stalkers, harassers and Internet trolls.[23]

1.) How do you feel about the number of people who truly know all of your stalking/harassment/Internet trolling experience and your current status?

2.) What discrepancies did you notice? Are there people you trust who do not know your experience? Are there people who are aware of the harassment, but with whom you do not feel close?

3.) Are there people on your list who have experienced online stalking, harassment or Internet trolling themselves? Have you reached out to them?

4.) Who in your family and extended family is on that list? Do you wish to change which list applies to them?

5.) If you have a therapist/mental health professional, which list are they on? Do you wish to change that?

6.) Carnes writes: "This list often reveals unfinished business that needs to be addressed or relationship work that needs to be done. **List any action steps you now need to take."** (emphasis added)

You've identified the important people in your life, taken a fresh look at how much they know about your stalking/harassment/Internet trolling situation, and outlined where you need to take action. In the next chapter, we'll continue looking outside of ourselves for another action step.

CHAPTER 14: ACT: SELFISH VS. SERVING

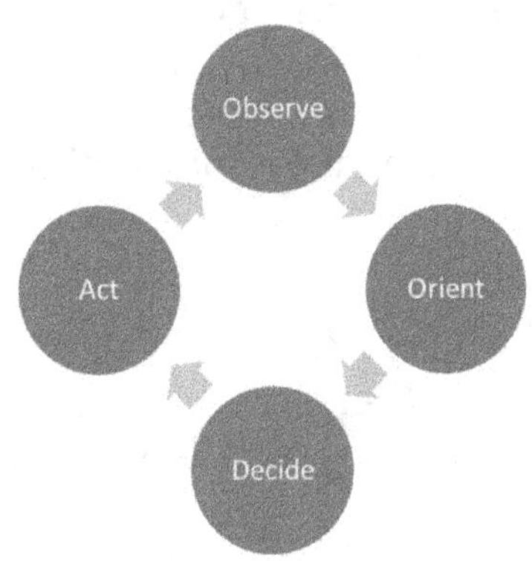

CHRIS trait: Selfishness

Online stalking, harassing and Internet trolling are self-centered acts. CHRIS might dress them up in rationalizations, but they're generally ugly underneath.

Karen's instigators could rationalize that they were striking a blow for the freedom against the "mask police," but most were just being cruel.

Gabby's troll Kelley Lynn cloaked her criticisms as just looking out for the taxpayer when it was really all about Kelley Lynn's own ego preservation and career salvation.

The Trap: Self-satisfaction

Together, we've spent the previous 13 chapters necessarily focused on our own thoughts, feelings and deeply held core beliefs. Even as we observed the hardships faced by others, we were simultaneously looking into a mirror of self-reflection.

There comes a point in your rebuilding-and-recovering journey at which you feel whole again. You may feel like your "old self" - but even stronger and more emboldened. Recall Gabby's bravado in Chapter 6 as one example.

Even as we express gratitude aloud to our personal support networks (Chapter 13), our ego might whisper to us that we won the war as an army of one. Having overcome our individual CHRISes, we can be subconsciously drawn into the same selfish personality that embodies our stalkers/harassers/Internet trolls.

The antidote: Service

The simplest way for us to avoid following CHRIS' selfish footsteps is to serve others. Just because that path is simple doesn't mean it's easy – especially when we're still early in recovery after the attack.

Specific and actionable tasks are outlined below. Each one enables you to practice the skills you've developed in the previous 12 chapters.

Journal

14.1 Using your Important People Inventory (Chapter 13), can you identify someone on your lists who has been or is currently dealing with online stalking/harassment/Internet trolling?

Have you asked them what you can do to support them? If the answer is no, why not? If yes, have you followed through?

14.2 Who in your broader social networks – online or in real life (IRL) - is dealing with online stalking/harassment/Internet trolling at this moment? Will you reach out to them? When?

14.3 "If you see something, say something." Can you

think of a recent occurrence where you witnessed stalking, harassment, or Internet trolling? What specifically would it take for you to reach out to a stranger going through that experience? When will you do it?

14.4 Every industry has members whose brush with the law has sent them to prison. In many cases, those individuals' legal status makes them a soft target for online dogpiling. Who in your industry has been publicly shamed, or dealt with online stalking/harassment/ Internet trolling, that is incarcerated? What would it take for you to reach out to them? When will you do it?

14.5 Over the past 14 chapters, you have executed all four steps of the Observe-Orient-Decide-Act (OODA) Loop. But you're not done yet. Remember, OODA is a loop because the steps are executed again and again.

As you have Observed, Oriented, Decided, and Acted, what have you learned about your own relationship with stalking, harassment, and Internet trolling behaviors that you want to change for the better?

When is the most recent time you have participated in stalking/harassment/Internet trolling behaviors?

Do you cheer your friends' unhealthy online behaviors out of loyalty?

When your friends are under attack, do you remain silent and hope their challenges go away? Do you see them reacting with excessive pride (Chapter 6) and choose to stroke their ego, potentially encouraging their self-destructive habits? Do you see how such enabling behavior could cause them to kill their highs and live by lows?

Use your journal to capture this snapshot of your present mindset and revisit your answers on your next OODA Loop.

CHAPTER 15: ACT: CLEANUP ON THE MILQUETOAST MAJORITY

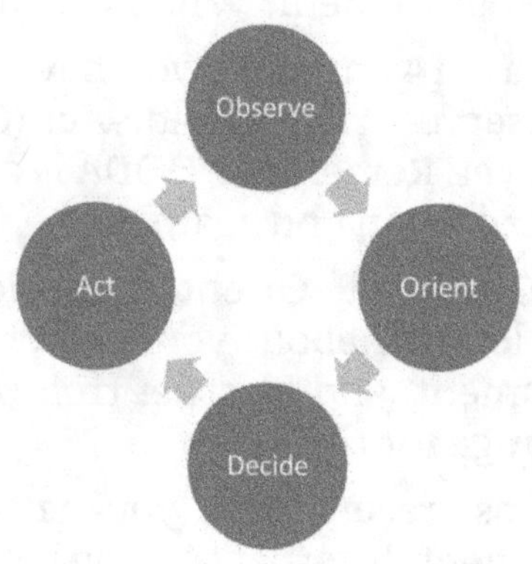

Can you forgive them?

No, not CHRIS. You're leaving that **S**talker/**H**arasser/**I**nternet **T**roll behind. If you believe forgiving your stalker is necessary to move forward, a mental health professional might be able to assist in that endeavor. For the purposes of this chapter, CHRIS is dying a lonely, painful death at the bottom of Stalker Sea, deprived of the oxygen of your attention.

In this moment, we're focusing on the Milquetoast Majority. All the people who saw you get attacked, maybe even heard about how much it affected you - and did nothing.

You might have a long history with some members of the Milquetoast Majority. Perhaps you attended college with them, worked at the same company or shared a pew at church. You attended their kids' birthday parties, contributed to their charity walks, and always left a "like" on their braggadocious social media posts.

And in your darkest hour, they were nowhere to be found.

Like Karen in Chapter 1, you feel abandoned. And like Lisa in Chapter 2, you wonder how they can go about their business as if you're not still hurting.

You were their friend when they needed you, but they didn't hold up their end of the bargain.

But was there ever really a bargain for them to uphold?

Covert contracts

If you're feeling hurt, angry, or disappointed over acquaintances' lack of support, there's a chance you were operating under a covert contract.

A covert contract is any arrangement in which you believe another person or group of people is obligated to behave toward you in a certain way, and the other party is unaware that the obligation exists. In other words, the "contract" exists only in your head.

Most everyone understands the dangers of unrealistic expectations, but covert contracts are more subtle, insidious and invade every aspect of our social lives.

- A passive-aggressive spouse performs extra household tasks or volunteers for non-traditional parenting duties in anticipation of earning a reward – maybe the freedom of a boys'/girls' weekend with friends or the right to overspend on a luxury item.
- An employee gives up vacation time or works extra

hours hoping company management will notice the sacrifice and award a bonus or promotion.

- A teenager improves his/her grades in the expectation of parents gifting desired electronics, a car, etc.

The overwhelming majority of covert contracts are ultimately unfulfilled. Why? We can't expect someone to uphold their end of a bargain if they don't even know the obligation exists.

Recalibrating expectations

It's not too much to expect friends to be there for us in a time of need. But before writing off someone completely, consider:

- Was this friend even aware of the attack on me? (Refer to the "Important People" exercise in Chapter 13.)
- Did I express to them the level of pain I was feeling, or did I expect them to read my mind?
- Is it possible this person thought that mentioning the stalking/harassment/Internet trolling to me would do more harm than good?
- Is my own definition of a friend too broad? Would it have been more accurate to describe this "friend" as an acquaintance all along?
- Was I operating under a covert contract with this person, expecting a minimum standard of engagement or support that he/she was unaware of?

Cleanup process

Hard feelings, sadness, general uneasiness. These are a few of the emotional packages we carry around inside our post-attack baggage.

In The Sedona Method, Hale Dwoskin outlines what Lester Levenson called the cleanup process. It's a series of steps originally designed to help Sedona Method trainers decompress and move on after teaching sessions. Dwoskin says the cleanup process can be used before, during and after every interaction we have, and can even be applied to people we no longer speak to or who have passed away.[24]

Use your journal as we move through the cleanup process to capture the thoughts and feelings that rise to your awareness.

Start with a Middling Milquetoast

Dwoskin recommends doing the first cleanup on a person for whom you do not have highly charged emotions – so start by identifying a person toward whom you have a noticeable, but not intense, resentment. You might pick an acquaintance you expected to reach out to you in your time of need, or stand up for you on social media, but they were absent or silent.

The cleanup process involves releasing on our core human wants (Chapter 8.) Dwoskin recommends a progression from control to approval to security. But since many stalking/harassment/Internet trolling attacks involve shaming (e.g., Karen in Chapter 1, Alyssa in Chapter 3) we'll modify Dwoskin's process and begin with approval.

Approval

Visualize a member of your Milquetoast Majority standing in front of you, then ask:

1.) Did it feel like this person disapproved of me after seeing/hearing the attack? Did it feel like they were withholding their approval?

2.) Could I let go of wanting approval from this person?

3.) Have I been withholding **my** approval from this person in response to **their** withholding of approval? Can I let go of disapproving of them, if only for this moment?

Continue releasing on this Milquetoast Majority member until you feel noticeably less **wanting** of their approval, and/or noticeably less **wanting** to express your disapproval of them.

Security

We've explored how CHRIS' attacks can affect our desire for security. That insecurity, or sense of wanting, can also affect how we view certain members of the Milquetoast Majority after the attack. Picture that same person from the approval exercise above, then ask:

1.) Did it feel like this person's absence or silence in my time of need was a threat to my security or my livelihood?

2.) Can I let go of wanting to feel a sense of security from this person?

3.) Have I been plotting ways to subtly undermine this person's security – their job, their family, their reputation – to make them feel what I felt? Can I let go of that desire to make them feel insecure, if only for this moment?

Continue releasing on this Milquetoast Majority member until you feel noticeably less **wanting** of the security they could provide, and/or noticeably less **wanting** to threaten their own security as payback.

Control

For some of us, our harshest distaste for the Milquetoast Majority centers on their inherent **disloyalty**. When we're operating under covert contracts, we are like children lining up toy soldiers for a pitched battle. How dare our friends and acquaintances not dutifully take up arms, visibly and publicly, when we are attacked!

Picture that same member of the Milquetoast Majority standing before you again, and ask:

1.) Did it feel like I deserved to direct this person's response to the attack on me?

2.) Did I attempt to send coded commands (e.g., via cryptic or emotional social media posts) to this person that were not received – or worse, received and ignored?

3.) Could I let go of wanting to control this person? Could I allow myself to accept this person as they are, without trying to control them?

Continue releasing on this Milquetoast Majority member until you feel noticeably less **wanting** to control them, and/or noticeably more **acceptance** of that person as they are today.

Co(vert) Dependent No More

Our ego reminds us that the Milquetoast Majority let us down once already. Those so-called "friends" could have taken up arms and stood shoulder-to-shoulder in solidarity as we battled our stalkers/harassers/Internet trolls – but instead, they were absent without leave.

Whether through covert contracts or unrealistic expectations, the fortress of our online persona was dismantled.

Pretending your feelings weren't injured is dishonest. Banishing every member of the Milquetoast Majority from your life is spiteful and could lead to crippling isolation.

Only through releasing on your desires for approval, security and control can you decide, case by case, who will remain, enter or depart your Important People network.

CHAPTER 16: THE CHARGE

We did not choose to be attacked by stalkers, harassers, and Internet trolls, but here we are.

We did not consent to the gutter war thrust upon us, but we will apply an airborne strategy to achieve our separate peace. We will **Observe** our own emotional reactions and actively release anxieties. We will **Orient** ourselves, examining core beliefs and feelings of self-worth, all while striving to eliminate our unquenchable thirsts for security, control and approval. We will reaffirm our **Decision** to improve our lives by improving our consciousness and take decisive **Action** to follow through.

As our individual and collective stalkers/harassers/ Internet trolls lay poisonous traps - daring us to ingest the venom that has infected their collective characters – we administer our own healing antidotes. We counter cowardice and heaviness with courage and lightness. We reject resentment and isolation, choosing gratitude and support. Ultimately, we transcend selfishness to serve.

CHAPTER 17: EPILOGUE

After some time has passed since you first completed the steps in this book, review the following checklist to see how much progress you've made.

As you tick through the checklist below, consider the gains you've made, as well as the areas where you still have room for improvement.

Observe

Yes/No

☐☐ When I'm triggered by a thought of my stalker/harasser/Internet troll experience, I pause and take time to identify which emotional level I'm on (my "right now" feeling.)

☐☐ After identifying my "right now" feeling, I stop, breathe, and begin the releasing process.

☐☐ As I release low-level emotions, I identify specific actions I can take to move higher up the emotional scale today.

Orient

☐☐ When I'm faced with a new attack – or when my mind is replaying an old one – I pause to let my

Observing Mind take over from my Monkey Mind.

☐☐ I use my Observing Mind to assess what aspect of my self-worth feels threatened by the attack.

☐☐ I distinguish between the actual content of the attack, and what I imagine is implied by the attack.

☐☐ When I'm faced with a new attack – or when my mind is replaying an old one – I identify which of my three main wants (control, security, approval) are at play.

☐☐ After I identify which of the wants I'm using to manufacture anxiety, I use the release technique to let go of those wants.

Decide

☐☐ Each day, I make a conscious decision to let go of the painful past and live my life utilizing the principles of recovery.

Act

☐☐ I demonstrate courage by closing the gap between my online identity and my true self.

☐☐ I do not dwell on past mistakes, nor do I deny how my actions may have invited chaos.

☐☐ I show up and am fully present in physical and virtual spaces that matter to me.

☐☐ Each day I demonstrate and take actions consistent with Courage, Acceptance and Peace.

☐☐ I focus on the gain – how far I've ascended from the lowest-frequency emotions – rather than the gap between where I am now and where I think I "should" be.

☐☐ I give thanks for gratitude-generating experiences before they happen.

☐☐ I overcome lingering self-destructive feelings of shame and embarrassment by sharing my experiences with trusted people, and with people going through their own stalking/harassment/Internet trolling experiences.

☐☐ I use my Important People Inventory to identify my support network and reassess the lists as my network grows.

☐☐ I share the tools and knowledge of recovery with others going through their own stalking/harassment/Internet trolling experiences.

☐☐ I use my elevated insight to identify my own stalking/harassment/Internet trolling behaviors,

behaviors, and those of my friends and acquaintances.

□□ I destroy lingering resentments by identifying my covert contracts.

□□ I actively release feelings of anger, hostility and resentment toward the Milquetoast Majority by freeing myself of the want for approval, security and control – and releasing my desires to disapprove of, threaten, and control them.

ACKNOWLEDGEMENTS

So You've Been Publicly Shamed by Jon Ronson is one of the two books I've sent most often to friends and acquaintances facing stalking, harassment and Internet trolling. The real-life case studies of people whose lives were turned upside down – and finally turned right-side-up – shows that the possibility of recovery and redemption is as real as the initial pain. Ronson's books are available at www.jonronson.com.

The other book I send most often to people struggling with online attacks is The Sedona Method. In addition to his books, Hale Dwoskin produces a weekly podcast, and provides e-mail updates at www.sedona.com.

I discovered the Sedona Method through Brian Begin's YouTube channel at youtube.com/TheFearlessMan. You can read more of Begin's content and learn about his products and programs at www.thefearlessman.com.

I first learned about the work of Dr. Joe Dispenza through the Aubrey Marcus podcast. Visit www.drjoedispenza.com for more.

JF Benoist's Addicted to the Monkey Mind: Change the Programming that Sabotages Your Life was a gift from AMB. Read more at www.jfbenoist.com.

I learned about John Boyd's OODA loop concept from Hedgeye Risk Management's Keith McCullough (specifically The Macro Show.) That's also where I learned about Dan Sullivan's The Gap and The Gain, referenced in the Epilogue checklist (Chapter 18.) Visit www.hedgeye.com to learn more.

I first heard about covert contracts from Rian Stone. His

blog is www.rianstone.com/blog, and his videos are at www.youtube.com/RianStone.

Finally, to the people who reached out to me in the summer of 2017 after seeing the attacks on me and my family: RA, AB, SB, RC, SF, AJ, CL, GM, TM, JR. I will always remember your kindness and thoughtfulness during the darkest days of my life. You have my unconditional and eternal gratitude.

REFERENCES

[1] Hale Dwoskin, "The Sedona Method," (Minnetonka, MN: Sedona Press, 2018.)

[2] "Your brain and body don't know the difference between an actual experience in your life and thinking about the experience – neurochemically, it's the same." – Dr. Joe Dispenza, "You are the Placebo" (Carlsbad, CA: Hay House, 2014.)

[3] An in-depth look at the search-engine results industry can be found in Jon Ronson's, "So You've Been Publicly Shamed," (New York: Riverhead Books, 2015.)

[4] Kelley Lynn's predicament is hardly unique; according to Syracuse University's Transactional Records Access Clearinghouse (TRAC) organization, United States Department of Justice records indicated 236 new official corruption prosecutions in the first six months of FY 2021 alone.

[5] Scott Adams, "The Joy of Work," (New York: Harper Paperbacks, 1998.)

[6] JF Benoist, "Addicted to the Monkey Mind: Change the Programming that Sabotages Your Life," (Pakalana Publishing, 2018.)

[7] Ibid.

[8] Ibid.

[9] Hale Dwoskin, “The Sedona Method,” (Sedona Press, Minnetonka, MN, 2018.)

[10] Ibid.

[11] Ibid.

[12] Ibid.

[13] Contact law enforcement if you have reason to believe you or others are in danger.

[14] Hale Dwoskin, “The Sedona Method,” (Sedona Press, Minnetonka, MN, 2018.)

[15]https://www.facebook.com/DrJoeDispenzaOfficialNewsFanPage

[16] As you complete this exercise, avoid blaming yourself when it is not warranted. Self-blaming is a common response when we are in the states of Apathy, Grief and Fear. Alyssa, for example, should not assign herself responsibility for James’ petulance after the breakup or for his vengeful and vindictive actions afterward.

[17] Brian Begin, “How To Release Emotions - The Basics Of Releasing - The Fearless Man,” https://www.youtube.com/watch?v=PVpzlE_dJZ8

[18] Hale Dwoskin, “The Sedona Method,” (Sedona Press, Minnetonka, MN, 2018.)

[19] UCLA Mindful Awareness Research Center at uclahealth.org/programs/marc

[20] Dr. Joe Dispenza, “Breaking the Habit of Being Yourself: How to Lose Your Mind and Create a New One,” (Hay House Inc., 2012.)

[21] Ibid.

[22] Dr. Patrick Carnes, "Facing the Shadow," (Gentle Path Press, 2001.)

[23] Ibid.

[24] Hale Dwoskin, "The Sedona Method," (Sedona Press, Minnetonka, MN, 2018.)

ABOUT THE AUTHOR

John Combest visited his first online message board in 1995 and became hooked on the Internet immediately. He designed his first webpage as a student at Washington University in St. Louis in 1999 and created his first website two years later.

In his 12 ½ years at a Fortune 500 company, John's diverse experiences included building corporate blogs, responding to misinformation campaigns, and crafting "executive voice" content (ghostwriting) for global leaders. These responsibilities provided an immersive environment to observe online attacks and the professional and personal havoc they can create.

Stalking, Harassment, Internet Trolling: A Guide to Recovering and Rebuilding After Online Attacks is his first book. Updates and additional resources can be found at facebook.com/johncombestauthor.

P.O. Box 512

Chesterfield, MO 63006

john@johncombestblog.com

www.ingramcontent.com/pod-product-compliance
Lightning Source LLC
LaVergne TN
LVHW051741050326
832903LV00029B/2659

* 9 7 9 8 9 8 7 3 3 8 9 1 9 *